Rethinking Teacher Education

Collaborative responses to uncertainty

Anne Edwards, Peter Gilroy
and David Hartley

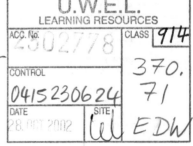

RoutledgeFalmer
Taylor & Francis Group

LONDON AND NEW YORK

First published 2002 by RoutledgeFalmer
11 New Fetter Lane, London EC4P 4EE

Simultaneously published in the USA and Canada
by RoutledgeFalmer
29 West 35th Street, New York, NY 10001

RoutledgeFalmer is an imprint of the Taylor & Francis Group

Typeset in Goudy and Gill by BC Typesetting, Bristol
Printed and bound in Great Britain by
TJ International Ltd, Padstow, Cornwall

British Library Cataloguing in Publication Data
A catalogue record for this book is available from the British Library

Library of Congress Cataloging in Publication Data
Edwards, Anne, 1946–
    Rethinking teacher education: collaborative responses to
uncertainty/Anne Edwards, Peter Gilroy, and David Hartley.
        p.   cm.
    Includes bibliographical references and index.
    1. Teachers–Training of–Philosophy. I. Gilroy, Peter.
II. Hartley, David, 1945– III. Title.

LB1707.E39 2002
370'71–dc21   2002073436

ISBN 0–415–23062-4 (hbk)
ISBN 0–415–23063–2 (pbk)

To my fathers David Gilroy and Dennis Francis (PG).

Contents

Tables and figures

Tables

Figures

Acknowledgements

We would like to thank Roger Osborn-King, Publisher of Triangle Journals Ltd, for his kind permission to allow us to use extracts from D. Hartley (2000) 'Shoring up the pillars of modernity: teacher education and the quest for certainty', *International Studies in Sociology of Education*, 10:2, 113–32.

Abbreviations

CACE	Central Advisory Council for Education
CATE	Council for the Accreditation of Teachers
CSE	Certificate in Secondary Education
CSILE	Computer Supported Intentional Learning Environments
DES	Department for Education and Science
DfEE	Department for Education and Employment
DfES	Department for Education and Skills
EU	European Union
GDP	Gross Domestic Product
ICT	Information and Communications Technology
LEA	Local Education Authority
NBPTS	National Board for Professional Teaching Standards
OECD	Organisation for Economic Co-operation and Development
OFSTED	Office for Standards in Education
OPEC	Organisation of Petroleum Exporting Countries
PDS	Professional Development Schools
TTA	Teacher Training Agency

Chapter 1

Three themes and one overview

Introduction

One of us, Peter Gilroy, recalls that he was recently teaching aspects of the work of Thomas Kuhn, author of the seminal *The Structure of Scientific Revolutions* on paradigm shifts. In talking about the psychological pain of living through a paradigm shift Gilroy suddenly realized that this description perfectly caught his own mood. He had previously put this down to some form of reverse culture shock. Having recently returned from a year's secondment to Singapore, he found that he was having considerable difficulty in settling back to his previous existence. He realized that what he was experiencing was a form of dissonance. That is to say, on the one hand he was researching and teaching the general field of the philosophy of change, with a particular focus on teacher education and professionalism, reaching conclusions about the contingent and shifting nature of knowledge in these fields. On the other hand he was living an academic life that involved him in a series of accommodations to the fact that teacher education, in England at least, was being fixed into apparent certainties. This recognition of what had been a tacit acceptance of academic contradictions is what bothered him. He came to the conclusion that, in effect, his professional life consisted of negotiating a series of ambivalences – and indeed outright contradictions – and it was this which was producing an uncomfortable feeling of inconsistency between what he professed through his teaching and writing and his lived experience in a department of teacher education.

This book is an attempt to describe, analyse and learn from sensations of dissonance in teacher education that all three authors are living through. We have each experienced teacher education in different ways. All of us are, or have recently been, involved in pre-service and in-service teacher education. We have also all engaged in research on teacher education as an object of study. However, to each of these experiences we bring our distinct histories as teachers and as researchers in psychology (Edwards), philosophy (Gilroy) and sociology (Hartley). We draw on these disciplines to try to make sense of current constructions of teacher education and where they might lead. But while our analyses are focused on past and present constructions of teacher education within their wider cultural contexts, they are driven by a desire to offer insights into how a rethought teacher education might address how teachers are positioned in relation to knowledge, learners, economic demands and democratic values.

In short, we suggest that any rethinking should take into account how teachers are helped to enable learners to contribute to the new knowledge economy and to societal well-being. That said, the substance of our analysis is framed by the official government discourse, especially that for teacher education, and especially that within England. That discourse is performative. It sets out the importance of fine-tuning education so that it resonates with the new economy. It sets great store by ensuring that education furthers national competitiveness within an increasingly globalized economy. But notwithstanding this attempt to render teacher education (and, by association, schooling) as functional for the economy, we are nevertheless mindful that the United Kingdom and other advanced economies are not only capitalist but also democratic. Whilst our central concern is to suggest that contemporary official policy for teacher education will do little for an emerging, knowledge-based economy, we shall say also that an overly bureaucratic, system-serving and standardized prescription admits little diversity, a diversity which an education system within a democracy should embrace and foster, not suppress. In sum, we shall argue, primarily, that current policy for schooling and teacher education will fail in its own terms.

That is, we know from work-based research that the employment relationship is changing from Fordist rigidities and overt supervision towards post-Fordist team-working, devolved responsibility, negotiation and self-supervision. Yet contemporary education policy clings to what are Fordist classroom processes which will be hardly functional for that new economy which requires greater flexibility and creativity. Nor – and this is very much a subsidiary thread in our analysis – will this adherence to Fordist classroom processes do much to enhance democracy by recognizing diversity or by questioning the inequalities which are sometimes buried within difference. That this is a subsidiary issue for us is not to diminish its importance. It is because official government discourses on curriculum and pedagogy are largely bereft of democratic ideals. Our concern is the official text, which we critique on its own economistic terms. Our rethinking, therefore, is stimulated by the kinds of dissonance we have just outlined. But it does not aim at a simple resolution of contradictions. Instead, the book has three major themes, which combine to challenge the simple certainties which are offered variously as the outcomes of and antidotes to the ambivalences and uncertainties with which teacher educators are living.

Theme one: policy, change and teacher education

Governments, perhaps by their very function, are drawn irresistibly towards certainties. They make policy. Politicians cluster around certainties like moths around a flame, accumulating them to create manifestos, policy documents and the paraphernalia of government. Over the last decade teacher education throughout the world has been at the receiving end of rafts of government initiatives which have been designed to bring order and control to education, a social institution which is central to a knowledge economy. Some of the tensions between policy certainty and lived uncertainty are outlined in a recent submission to the OECD: 'What is emerging from our analysis is the vision of an extraordinarily dynamic, flexible, productive economy, together with an unstable, fragile society, and an increasingly insecure individual' (Carnoy and Castells, 1997: 53).

Work, the family and society are undergoing profound changes. Education – and, by implication, teacher education – must make sense of these shifts. The changing of teacher education is a well-established project. In the USA the Holmes Group was formed in 1986 in order to provide a forum for university teacher educators in the wake of the criticism levied in President Reagan's *A Nation at Risk* publication. In Australia the Howard government is transforming the higher education system; in France teacher education has been radically overhauled; and, of course, the government's reforms of teacher education in England and Wales have become a byword for rapid and radical change.

One feature that appears to be common to many of these government-driven changes is the lack of any substantial rational support for them, other than perhaps the rationale of the market. Their agenda are offered in a discourse marked by transcendental certainties that find expression in a series of anti-teacher-educator slogans that do little but capture an ideology in a sound-bite. Such slogans associate teacher education variously with the dangerous left, with out-of-touch academics and profligate wastage of public funds. It matters little that rational arguments can be advanced to show that such emotive statements have little purchase on reality, and are even self-contradictory. The purpose of such statements is not to play a part in the discourse of rationality but rather to take a leading role in the language of political debate.

Indeed, teachers, the very people who might have been expected to defend postgraduate training and the status it brings, chose to opt out of the fray. Why has teacher education failed to bring teachers to its defence? One response may be that offered by Bottery and Wright, who suggest that teachers lack a structural awareness of the conditions which frame their professional existence (Bottery and Wright, 1999). Doubtless teacher educators are in part culpable here. In an important sense both teacher educators and politicians have been talking past each other in a language that neither understands nor identifies with. The UK government's dominant discourse for teacher education is one of simple common sense. But teacher education, like any other professional endeavour, is complex. Yet this complexity, when it is expressed by teacher educators, is dismissed by government as just academic, bereft of what works, bereft of common sense. Teacher educators are being forced to simplify what is eminently complex and are therefore victims of what David Hartley (1997) calls a *discourse of duplicity*, while teachers watch from the sidelines, disengaged from battles between the advocates of simplicity and complexity.

Theme two: the loss of disciplines' certainty

One of the many challenges that has to be faced by teacher educators attempting to develop a teacher education which works with and on complexity is how to deal with the fact that the underlying assumptions of the foundation disciplines (psychology, philosophy, history, sociology) have changed. Until, say, the mid-1970s, the disciplines were sure of their pre-eminent position in teacher education. Although they may not have appeared especially relevant to the immediate practical concerns of schoolteachers, they were seen by many as providing a sound theoretical base to the practice of education, none more so than the psychology of education. Why, then, have the disciplines not taken a more active part in identifying what is valuable and unique to their contribution to teacher education?

One possible answer to this question is that the deafening silence from the foundation disciplines is a direct result of their bluff having been called. As emperors *sans* clothes it could be said that they have no defence to make because they offer no meaningful contribution to teacher education. However, we suggest it is useful to think of teacher education which is *for the practice of teaching*, on the one hand, and teacher education which is *about the institution of education*, on the other. It is the psychology of education which has attended most to the former *for teaching* issues, whilst the history, philosophy and sociology of education have provided the disciplinary basis for matters *about education*. In the reforms of teacher education in the UK in the 1980s and 1990s, these *about education* issues have been given short shrift, whilst the *for teaching* issues have gained prominence. However, in England at least, these *for teaching* concerns in teacher education have been relocated, to be addressed in schools where they are to be found in versions of craft knowledge which are rarely informed by psychology as a discipline.

But another way of responding is to say that the so-called foundation disciplines which inform teacher education are themselves undergoing a radical change: their previous certainties are seen as being irrelevant to the changed theoretical world. From that response follows the argument that current and developing versions of the foundation disciplines do have something to offer teacher education. Indeed, teacher education may operate usefully as a site where a broad spectrum of the social sciences play together to offer close-to-practice versions of their disciplines informed by the rules, meanings, beliefs and actions of their playfellows.

Working at the margins of one's discipline in an applied field in collaboration with other disciplines may, however, jeopardize one's position as a member of a disciplinary community. Some of these communities are more able to accommodate changing identities than are others. But, more often than not, educational versions of the foundation disciplines occupy a low status within their home disciplines and are therefore likely to have little impact on them. The comfortable certainties that once delineated the disciplines of history, philosophy, psychology and sociology in education have disappeared, leaving behind educational researchers and teacher educators grappling with ambivalent academic identities. Reactions to this instability have included their choosing to work in other fields, building strong alliances with home disciplines or recognizing that education as a field of study and a site of intervention can benefit from multidisciplinary insights.

In a sense, this disruption of disciplinary purity is simply a sign of contemporary culture. Culture in contemporary society is such that it weakens the purity of categories and identities. Consumer culture spawns many choices. Disciplines are the intellectualization of this culture, and we should not be surprised that their purity has been contaminated and new forms allowed to develop. Some philosophers may take an epistemological perspective, arguing that the disciplines represent *logically* different ways of understanding – ways of understanding which are culture-free. However, that is not the line we are pursuing. Instead, our second theme explores how working at disciplinary margins in multidisciplinary enquiry may allow us to see fresh horizons and possibilities which can inform teacher education and our changing relationships with knowledge.

Teacher educators, we suggest, are caught up in the identity shifts and adjustments at disciplinary boundaries in the academy. Equally, they are open to the criticism from quick-fix politicians that they, as academics in ivory towers, have nothing certain to say about the theoretical basis of practice. How can one answer the certainty of the politician with the tentative response of the professional who is dealing with complexities? Poised uncomfortably between the horns of a dilemma – of speaking out in support of a discipline, or of accepting that traditional conceptions of what constitutes a discipline have changed – it is tempting to say nothing. Here then is another source of dissonance, in that teacher educators know that what they do is of value, but they cannot easily articulate that value.

Theme three: the paradox of uncertainty

What can fill the vacuum of the discipline's certainty? One answer that we explore is that an understanding of the nature of knowledge might well provide some sort of base from which to identify where certainty might lie. Such an enquiry leads sooner or later into arguments advanced by postmodernists, one of whose central assumptions is that in living through uncertainties it is possible simply to accept the confusions, contradictions, paradoxes and inconsistencies that inevitably arise in such an age. There are at least two ways of addressing this assumption. The first is to point out that this is our 'natural' state and that it is up to teacher educators to find ways to accommodate to such an age. One example of this approach, following the work of Schön, would be the attempts by teacher educators to find ways in which the conception of teachers' practical knowledge can provide some sort of flexible foundation for building a tentative home for their expertise as teacher educators. There is an obvious tension here, for no matter how one attempts to qualify that knowledge-base, it still appears to hark back to some sort of modernism. The challenge is to avoid notions of a 'knowledge-base' which are synonymous with simple fixed certainties, but to consider how teachers relate to the contestable and shifting knowledge available to them.

Another approach is to analyse carefully what kinds of certainty and uncertainty are being offered as representing modernism and post-modernism. Here, *postmodernity* is taken to be a chronological term, the age beyond the modern – indeed we are also inclined to the terms late capitalism or late modernity. *Postmodernism* is taken to be the cultural expression of contemporary capitalism; *postmodernist* (or *post-modernist theory*) is taken to be an anti-representationalist argument (not a theory) of two kinds: first, the pessimistic and nihilistic post-modernists who reflect in the dark abyss; second, the optimistic or critical postmodernists who use deconstructionism as a means to a political (or emancipatory) purpose. Later, we take *neo-Fordism* to be the flexible management style which is increasingly to be found within some sectors of the globalized economy. There are barely charted epistemological waters here, and in the absence of any substantial critique it is naturally tempting to assume that there is a simple dichotomy between the two positions (modernist and postmodernist theory), rather than a more complex relationship. It is this combination of an unexamined understanding of how to operate *qua* teacher educator, in a period of radical cultural shifts which are still not understood, coupled to a lack of understanding of quite what the relationship is between modernity and postmodernity, that provides another source of dissonance.

Overview

We intend to address these three themes as sources of the dissonance teacher educators experience directly.

Chapter 2, *Political and economic uncertainty and teacher education*, locates teacher education within the emerging redefinition of the welfare state and the new managerialism. In particular it explores two paradoxes: first, that between diversity of providers and the centralization of curriculum; and second, that between the globalization of markets and the resurgence of nationalism as a cultural phenomenon. How will teacher education position itself in relation to these paradoxes?

More generally, the chapter considers what 'flexibility' shall mean for teachers and for teacher educators.

Chapter 3, *Philosophical uncertainty and teacher education*, starts with the proposition that some sort of knowledge is passed on during the process of teacher education, and this chapter identifies issues raised by the epistemological justification for such knowledge. In particular it identifies the way in which the full range of teachers' continuing professional development (from initial teacher education through to post-experience) can be represented as a battlefield where the modernist and postmodernists meet to resolve and fight out their different interpretations of the nature of knowledge in teacher education. The dichotomy between these two extremes is resolved by an epistemology based on the notions of 'lived uncertainty' and the 'collaborative professional' (as opposed to the 'reflective practitioner'), which also allows for the missing value element of teacher education to be reintroduced to the debate concerning the nature of teacher education. The remaining chapters address the issue of how this uncertainty can be dealt with.

Chapter 4, *Modernist policy solutions*, describes and analyses how, since 1979, in Britain, and more latterly in other countries, the professions within the welfare state have had to do more with less. In some countries teachers have been blamed for a lack of economic competitiveness with the emergent Pacific-rim economies, and international league-table data on standards of mathematics and science have underlined what is seen as an underperformance by the more traditional capitalist economies. Back-to-basics and what-works solutions – both devoid of theory – have been imposed by governments. Reviews of teacher education by central governments (as in England and Wales), by the profession itself (the Holmes Group reports) or by independent think-tanks, have all caught teacher education in their gaze. These solutions have sought to render certain the uncertainties dealt with in Chapter 2. Examples are drawn from England and Wales (CATE and the TTA) and from the United States (the Holmes Group).

In Chapter 5, *Psychology: an agent of modernity in teacher education?*, we explore the following topics: how psychology has positioned itself as an agent of modernity by providing a rationale for governments' modernizing projects in education; how psychology might be most usefully critiqued; and how a more hermeneutic version of psychology might support teachers as they interpret and respond to the demands of practice. Throughout these analyses lies a concern with supporting teachers as they construct and use the intellectual and social resources available to them. To that end it is argued that multidisciplinary work may be usefully carried out in partnerships between education professionals in order to strengthen the field, professionals within it and teacher education.

Chapter 6, *Collaborative responses to uncertainty*, asks 'how might teacher education respond to the need to create learners able to generate as well as use knowledge?' Ensuring that teaching is not limited to promoting passive regurgitation calls for informed responsible teachers, who are able to make choices when helping learners to use the resources available to them. It demands a capacity to work with rather than avoid uncertainty. Parallel demands are therefore made on initial training and continuing professional development. The question is answered by invoking sociocultural interpretations of teaching and learning which see relationships between learners, teachers, knowledge and contexts as a dynamic weaving together of opportunities and constraints which shape both teaching and learning.

Chapter 7 is *Rethinking teacher education*. Here we attempt to bring together the strands of what a new teacher education might look like. It begins with a brief restatement of the argument in Chapter 6. We go on to suggest why, now, this will resonate at one and the same time with contemporary culture *and* with an emergent neo-Fordist work regime within an increasingly service-sector economy. Whilst the disciplinary purists and quick-fix, certainty-seeking politicians may have little truck with our conclusion – that is to say, we do not seek to proselytize *a big-t Truth* for teacher education – we suggest that teaching, in a culturally and intellectually complex society, cannot be reduced to neat solutions which the tidy-minded can live with. We end with the implications of our arguments for teacher professionalism and a final chapter, Chapter 8, *Delivering deliverance*, with David Hamilton providing a response to our pursuit of the three themes which structure our book.

Chapter 2

Political and economic uncertainty and teacher education

The chapter locates teacher education within the emerging redefinition of the welfare state and the new managerialism. In particular it explores two paradoxes: first, that between diversity of providers and the centralization of curriculum; and second, that between the globalization of markets and the resurgence of nationalism as a cultural phenomenon. How will teacher education position itself in relation to these paradoxes? More generally, the chapter considers what 'flexibility' shall mean for teachers and for teacher educators.

Teacher education seems to be pulled in different directions, enmeshed in different discourses, revealing different influences. These influences are economic, cultural and intellectual. The purpose of this chapter is to explore the first two of these influences and to introduce the third. By economic influences, we mean increasing economic globalization; and, with it, curbs in many countries on levels of expenditure on the welfare state. We see also new modes of governance and management within the agencies of the welfare state, including education. By cultural influences, we mean that culture which often attracts the term postmodernism, or – as it is sometimes called – the culture of consumerism. These cultural influences intersect with economic ones. Finally, teacher education is necessarily enmeshed within the so-called 'foundation' disciplines which inform it. In this chapter, as a preface to the next, we merely introduce the rifts and ructions which have begun to disturb – some would say even undermine – the once-firm intellectual foundations (philosophy, psychology, sociology, history) of teacher education. But it must be stressed that, although we consider these different influences in turn, none can stand apart from the others. They are related. Furthermore, the order in which they are defined here is by no means one which sets out a causal direction from the economic to the intellectual. Nevertheless, we suggest that there are affinities among them, and that contemporary capitalism allows for some cultural, intellectual and political forms to emerge more easily than others.

The economic context of teacher education: globalization

Capitalism is being restructured on a global scale. Transnational corporations constantly seek to increase their profitability by relocating to those parts of the world where the rate of return on their investment is maximized. Capital now flows around the world almost instantaneously, in digital form, without regard for national boundaries. Speculators can cause a run on a currency which a national government can do little to prevent. The Pacific-rim economies have been developing rapidly. Whilst they are currently experiencing something of an economic downturn, in the longer term we can expect much competition from them. And they have access to capital, to an educated labour force, to very low wage-levels and to vast domestic markets; nor are they overly burdened by the costs of a welfare state. They are in business, in competition among themselves, and with the more mature economies of the west.

During the 1980s, in the west, governments viewed with alarm the rise of the economies in the east, especially the Japanese economy. President Reagan, for example, attributed the weakened condition of America's economy to its education system. His influential Report – published in 1983, and widely copied elsewhere – was entitled *A Nation at Risk* (National Commission on Excellence in Education, 1984). President Clinton was to follow it with *Goals 2000*. In the United States national standards continue to be seen as the saviour of a fractured nationalism and as a reviver of a declining competitiveness within global markets (Ravitch, 1997).

This interesting mix of nationalism and millennialism has proved to be a popular one. Throughout the developed nations governments have been busily urging us towards efficiency and excellence. Take another example: the White Paper published by the Scottish Office (1997) entitled *Raising the Standard*. Here the term 'standard' has an intended double meaning. The implication is that those who would take issue with this policy will at a stroke undermine economic competitiveness and national pride. Who, therefore, would wish to be accused of lowering the standard? Or consider England and Wales: in the 1980s child-centred pedagogy had come to be regarded as near-heresy. It was said to have lured schoolteachers off their true course, taking them on a detour of pedagogical deviation, causing primary education in particular to have lost its way. The National Curriculum and OFSTED were to return them to good teaching. Echoing the United States' *Nation at Risk* discourse in its *National Curriculum 5–16* (DES, 1987), the Department for Education and Science put it plainly: 'We must raise standards consistently, and at least as quickly as they are rising in competitor countries' (para. 6). All these emotive appeals to nationhood and competition have something of a Darwinist ring to them, and they echo a former appeal which was made in 1957 when the Russian *Sputnik* satellite caused a root-and-branch reform of science education in the United States. Now, of course, it is not military destruction which awaits us if we don't pull our socks up – it is economic destruction. But what has focused the minds of policy-makers have been a series of international standardized tests in mathematics and in science. Consider some of the results of the *International Mathematics and Science Survey for 1998–1999* (IEA, 2000) (Table 1). Thirty-eight countries participated. England and the USA are coasting along quietly in the middle range. The newly emerged Asian economies cluster around the top of the table. This is regarded by some politicians as not being good enough. The assumption is that there is a causal relationship between these scores and economic development. But much controversy

Table 1 International comparisons in mathematics and science at Grade 8, national score 1999

	Mathematics	Science
Singapore	604 [1]	568 [2]
Japan	579 [5]	550 [4]
Korea	587 [2]	549 [5]
Australia	525 [11]	540 [7]
Canada	531 [10]	533 [14]
New Zealand	491 [21]	510 [19]
Netherlands	540 [7]	545 [6]
England	496 [20]	538 [9]
USA	502 [19]	515 [18]
Slovak Republic	534 [8]	535 [11]

Note: figures in brackets denote rank order out of 38 countries

surrounds these data (Galton, 1998). All we wish to say is that these surveys have been used as a ready excuse for governments to intervene in education so as to forge a tighter bond between education and economy. Needless to say, it is the teachers – and those who train them – who have been brought to book.

Economic globalization and education

The emerging globalization and interdependence of markets raises an interesting question: can we expect to see also the emergence of common structures and functions in education on a global basis? If we argue that what counts as education is itself a cultural artefact, contingent upon time and place, then it is reasonable to suggest that, as markets and consumer culture become more globalized, so too will what counts as education. But if one were to raise this possibility one might be well advised to prepare for a clamour of assertions about national identity and education. The Scots, for example, would say that their education system – like their legal system – is quite different from that in England. The Welsh Assembly is now responsible for education in Wales. The English, of course, made much of their National Curriculum, which was legislated in 1987. And is it not true that in many parts of the world ethnic groups are staking their claims to separate statehood: the Québécois, the Basques, the Corsicans – to name but a few? So there seems to be a paradox: whilst there is an increasing amount of economic interdependence, there is nevertheless good evidence that nationhood is asserting itself.

Let us consider this further. Why is it that many nation states are structurally similar on many unexpected dimensions, but yet change in unexpectedly similar ways (Meyer et al., 1997: 145)? Meyer et al. dismiss two common explanations of nation states. The first explanation is what they term the macrorealist argument. Put simply, nation states are the product of worldwide systems of economic power, exchange and competition (p. 147). The second explanation, termed microrealist, argues that nation states are social constructions which are locally and historically situated: that is, there are no macro structural forces coming into play. They go on to argue, however, that 'nation-states exhibit a great deal of isomorphism in their structures and policies' (p. 152). By isomorphism they mean a complementarity in the forms and functions of the state, which includes education. Imagine, for example, a set of Russian dolls, which nest inside each other, complementary in form, but different in size. This is not to state that structures and policies are as one, but that, for the most part, there is very little variation:

> In world culture, almost every aspect of social life is discussed, rationalized, and organized, including rules of economic production and consumption, political structure, and education; science, technique and medicine; family life, sexuality, and interpersonal relations; and religious doctrines and organizations. In each arena, the range of legitimately defensible forms is fairly narrow.
>
> (Meyer *et al.*, 1997: 162)

They stress that what is common to most nation states is a tendency to rationalize the forms and functions of government and its agencies (p. 167). An example of this is the OECD's *Common Framework for Country Reports on Issues and Developments in Public Management – Survey 1996–1997* (OECD, 1998a). The criteria converge. It is not so much now a matter of national standards as of global standards.

Let us elaborate upon these. Among them are: constitutional forms centred upon the rights of the individual and state power; mass schooling with very similar curriculum and pedagogy; rationalized data-collection systems; birth control policies; equal opportunities policies; environmental policies; universal welfare systems; standardized definitions of health and disease; and increasing privatization and marketization of education (Meyer *et al.*, 1997: 152–3). Even the ways in which national cultural forms are depicted – in tourism and in museums, for example – are of a piece. They go on to comment:

> Theories reasoning from the obviously large differences among national economies and cultural traditions have great difficulty accounting for these observed isomorphisms, but they are sensible outcomes if nation-states are enactments of the world cultural order.
>
> (Meyer *et al.*, 1997: 153)

By this 'world cultural order', they mean a highly rationalized one. And the 'rationalized actor' can refer to an individual, to an organization or even to a nation state. The 'mind-set' will be similar. Perhaps one of the earliest forms of rationalized behaviour was that expected of us in bureaucracies – that 'iron cage of bureaucratic rationality', as Max Weber termed it. One of the most elaborate bureaucratic procedures in manufacturing attracted the term 'Fordism', after Henry Ford, the mass-producer of cars in Detroit during the 1920s. Fordism rests on the following principles: first, standardized products which allow for standardized production methods, which in turn allow for economies of scale; second, purpose-built machinery which will be dedicated to the task of producing the said standardized products; third, the application of Taylorist management theory whereby tasks are broken down into their component sub-tasks, thereby allowing for the close monitoring of time-on-task and overall throughput; and fourth, the moving assembly line, which regulates the flow of sequentially ordered tasks. Fordism is most appropriate under the following conditions: a stable consumer market; a stable product with well-understood raw materials and technologies; large stock-piles of materials; a rigidly bureaucratic organizational form, strongly hierarchical, with highly specified routines for every facet of production; and, finally, an adherence to Keynesian economics whereby the state would intervene in order to regulate supply and demand. None of these principles and practices turned on the ownership of the means of production: they were as agreeable to the Soviets in the 1920s as they were to their American capitalist counterparts. The Holocaust was a tragic example of the mass-production of death. And this is the point which Meyer *et al.* would stress: what is important is not the ownership of the means of production but the very efficiency of this highly rationalized way to mass-produce or to mass-murder. A recent and popular reconsideration of this is Charles Ritzer's book *The McDonaldization of Society* (1993).

Rationalization is central to modernity. Since the dawn of the Enlightenment in the late eighteenth century we have sought to make sense of the world, theoretically. The social, mental and physical domains have all been subjected to the scientific endeavour. We have assumed that if we can understand the world, then we can go on to change it, for the better. This is what we mean by progress. But – and it is a big 'but' – science has not given us an overarching world-view in the way that, say, a magical or religious world-view has done. These latter world-views give us answers to questions such as 'Why are we here?' and 'How shall we live our lives?' Science, however, cannot sort out our moral dilemmas. And science tends to cool the emotions. We become detached; we purport to be rational actors, cool operators. All the same, one cannot deny the great strides which science has made in our understanding of the natural world. But at issue is Meyer *et al.*'s point that world society is rationalizing rapidly, and it is the professions who comprise the new secular priesthood, for their 'rationalized knowledge structures constitute the religion of the modern world' (p. 166). In education, for example, examples of this kind of knowledge would include behaviourism as a theory of cognition, or the aims-and-objectives approach to curriculum development, or checklists of competences.

By the late 1960s the 'mass' of modernity began to look too burdensome, and it began to be undermined. The certainties and stabilities of mass-production and consumption seemed dated, dysfunctional. Long-adhered-to patterns of consumption and compliance began to fragment. The resistance of organized trade unions became more marked, allegedly diminishing levels of profitability and investment. To all this was added the OPEC oil embargo which resulted in a near-fourfold increase in the price of oil. In the 1970s an industrial recession ensued. Meanwhile it began to emerge that in Japan – especially in the Toyota company – new kinds of production process were in train. The efficiency gains were reportedly considerable. By contrast, production practices in the United States and Europe looked decidedly sclerotic.

This brings us to post-Fordism and its interrelated elements. These are: its technology (robotics and computers); its production processes and organizational structure (re-engineering; total quality management; just-in-time manufacturing; zero-defect policies; flat hierarchies and franchising); its core and peripheral flexible workers; its material and cultural products; its globalization (the transnational corporations); and its social deficits (high unemployment and insecurity). Put generally, post-Fordism is said to accord with flexible specialization (Hirst and Zeitlin, 1991: 2). This is to be contrasted with mass-production in that flexible specialization 'can be defined as the manufacture of a wide and changing array of customized products using flexible, general-purpose machinery and skilled, adaptable workers'. Hirst and Zeitlin make three further important points. First, mass-production is not inherently inferior because this kind of evaluation has to be made in relation to the market environment of the organization. That is to say, a stable product in a stable environment would be more efficiently produced using mass-production techniques; on the other hand, a fast-changing market might be better served by a flexible specialization mode, one better able to cope with the demand for customized products. Second, they suspect that firms opt neither for one form nor the other, preferring to keep their options open (p. 6). Third, they suggest that it is somewhat tempting to link post-Fordist work processes with post-modernist culture (which is considered in the next section), thereby presenting an interpretation of society which is fluid not fixed, which is individualistic not collectivistic, which is consumerist and service-oriented rather than focused on production, which emphasizes style not substance, and which is marked by interest-driven politics rather than by mass movements (p. 11). At the same time, as we have said, other economies in Asia – Taiwan, Korea and Malaysia – have begun to develop rapidly. Like the west, they had a well-educated workforce and access to capital. Unlike the west, however, tax-rates were low in the absence of a welfare state, and they were not burdened by a weakening work ethic and trade union movement.

Within teacher education, post-Fordism may portend new modes of regulation of both teachers and teacher educators. Of the former, it may portend an increasing casualization of teachers' work, with the power of headteachers increasing as performance-related schemes and their variants come into play. Deference may increase, diversity may decrease as 'best-practice' teaching is defined by officialdom. Pay-bargaining deals may be cut locally, not nationally. Of the latter, governments – be they at regional or at national levels – may put down standards for teacher education 'providers'; and these providers may include for-profit corporations who act under contract. Spatially, teacher education may be transformed: first, through the breaching of boundaries between provider and school, linking the two (or more, as a network); and second, through virtual pedagogical spaces made possible by ICT. Temporally, teacher education will have no definable end-state, for continuing professional development (and accreditation) will be required. The vocabulary of the new teacher education may come to resonate with both economic shifts (the need for rigorous and recognizable standards in order to maximize global competition, and to ensure 'best value') and with cultural shifts (the emphasis on a sense of ownership, on team-work and on empowerment).

The reform of the welfare state

The debate about the welfare state has turned on a question: does a well-developed welfare state minimize a nation's capacity to be competitive? Drawing upon Esping-Andersen's (1996) conceptualization of welfare regimes, Gough (1996) underlines the complexity of the issue. In 'liberal welfare regimes', such as the USA, the UK and New Zealand, Gough argues that the dominant threats to productivity are 'instability in demand, a poor quality educational base and social disintegration' (p. 227). The new Labour government in the UK has now set about improving the second of these, but unless levels of poverty are reduced, and unless the rate of community disintegration is reversed, productivity gains will be difficult. In 'conservative welfare regimes' – typically those found in, say, France or Germany – high social security costs cannot always be paid for by increased productivity, so public sector deficits will increase. Here, argues Gough, there are indeed indications of a negative correlation between welfare expenditure and productivity. There is a third welfare regime – 'social democratic regimes', as in Sweden and Denmark. Here inequality is low, and taxation rates are high, as are non-wage costs for employers. But overall employment rates are high, as is productivity. Of these three regimes, Gough suggests that the third is the most likely to achieve a rational solution to the demands for welfare spending and the ability to pay for it through increased productivity. Castells sees little room for manoeuvre:

> Since firms, because of information technology, can locate in many different sites and still link up to global production networks and markets . . . there follows a downward spiral of social costs composition . . . In an economy whose core markets for capital, goods and services are increasingly integrated on a global scale, there is little room for vastly different welfare states, with relatively similar levels of labour productivity and production quality.
>
> (Castells, 1997a: 253)

By the mid-1970s doubts were already being expressed about the postwar settlement in education. On the political left, the view was that the egalitarian measures of the 1950s and 1960s had still left the same kinds of pupils winning and losing in the educational race. Tinkering about with the education system – however well intentioned – could not much ameliorate the disadvantaging effects of a class-ridden society. In England, for example, it was argued that both comprehensive schools and the policy of positive discrimination, whilst very much to be welcomed, did not go far enough. For the radical left, the answer was to socialize the means of production. But the left was divided. In 1976, a Labour prime minister, James Callaghan, wavered in his adherence to egalitarian and socialist principles. At Ruskin College, Oxford, aided and abetted by his mandarins, he began to call teachers to account. And 'account' is a central concept in the reform of teacher education now being administered in England. This is so because the welfare state, of which education is a part, is said to be in a state of fiscal overload, a victim of its own success, with rising expectations and declining tax revenues to pay for them.

On the political right, the faction known as the New Right saw the seeds of moral and economic decline being sown in so-called progressive primary schools and in comprehensive secondary schools. Some well-publicized schools – William Tyndale School in London, for example – were held up as exemplars of ineffective schools. Whilst education for the individual was said to be all to the good, it must not be at the expense of education for the economy. The work ethic was said to have been discarded by many in favour of the me-too consumerism being pushed by the advertisers through the now-pervasive medium of television. For the New Right there was work to be done. Basics – Victorian ones at that – were to be brought back; teachers were called to account, particularly over so-called progressive methods, and there were calls for more rigorous inspection of schools in Callaghan's Ruskin speech.

The welfare state had been too successful. The more health and education we received, the more we desired. Demand was exponential, but the ability to pay for it was said not to be. Nor could those in the United Kingdom continue to exploit the Commonwealth. The colonies were being off-loaded at a rapid rate. And, to make matters worse, the competition from the east was beginning to look very stiff indeed. In 1979 the British electorate voted for the solution offered by the Conservative Party. Under Thatcherism there were to be no alternatives. Competition was to be restored. The market was to be set free. Organized labour was to be undermined. The social wage was to be cut. The private was set to prevail over the public. The consumer was primed to prod the provider into service. Whereas before the consumer took what was on offer from the supplier, now the supplier was to provide what the consumer demanded. 'Producer capture' was no longer an option. The customer was both to be informed and to be privileged. Even so, what the consumer desired was not necessarily to be left entirely to the consumer. The consumer's desires could be designed to fit the material and cultural products of the advertisers, who themselves were hired by producers. In all this, sophisticated market research became an essential procedure. The consuming public were to be very finely categorized, and thereafter targeted. Credit card transactions left a digital trail, which could be analysed in order to discern patterns. Colour, space, sounds and texture would all be co-ordinated to generate integrated styles of consumption.

The welfare state, including education, was to be managed in a new way. In the New Public Management of the welfare state, central government increasingly appropriated strategic control of the ends of education, devolving to local authorities and (especially) to schools the 'ownership' of the tactics whereby these ends would be achieved. And, if not, then financial penalties would be applied; or, more radically, certain duties would be contracted out on a fee-for-service basis. Whereas before government funding of education was seen as an investment, up-front, now it came to be seen as a reward for meeting specified targets. The OECD (1998a: 15) summarizes the shift as being:

> a focus on results of efficiency, effectiveness, quality of service and whether the intended beneficiaries actually gain;

> a decentralised management environment which better matches authority and responsibility so that decisions on resource allocation and service delivery are made closer to the point of delivery, and which provide scope for feedback from client and other interest groups;

> a greater client focus and provision for client choice through the creation of competitive environments with and between public sector organizations and non-government competitors;

> the flexibility to explore more cost-effective alternatives to direct public provision or regulation, including the use of market type instruments, such as user charging, vouchers and the sale of property rights; and

> accountability for results and for establishing due process rather than compliance with a particular set of rules, and a related change from risk avoidance to risk management.

In sum, bureaucracy is being moved. It is being pushed down the line from central government to the level of the institution. This new mode of rationalization accords well with Meyer et al.'s predictions. With it has come a completely new vocabulary in education: efficiency, choice, effectiveness, excellence, targets, standards, monitoring, audits, plans, appraisal, relevance and entrepreneurship. The discourse of humanism and democracy, so typical of the 1950s and 1960s, has been either set aside or reworked so that these market reforms have a democratic ring to them. For example, the widespread use of the terms 'choice' and 'devolution' sound democratic, but – as research now shows – their aggregative effects are to produce more, not less, inequality (Whitty et al., 1998).

The neo-liberal governance of education in Britain – especially in England and Wales – has revealed a paradox: whilst government has sought to maximize the available choice of schools, it has also minimized the range of curricular content by specifying a national curriculum. Only the provider, not the product, is open to market forces. So it is a rigged market; or, as Glennerster (1991) suggests, a 'quasi-market'. Whilst it is too early to say whether or not this mode of governance will serve as a global paradigm – our earlier discussion of Meyer et al.'s ideas would suggest it might – it has nevertheless gained considerable ground, and so far it has offered little room for manoeuvre. Although teacher educators have encouraged teachers to 'give voice' to their concerns, the teacher educators themselves have been curiously reluctant to do so, though there have been some important exceptions (Gilroy, 1992).

So markets and standards work together. That is to say, there must be an objective way for consumers to distinguish between providers. This requires standardized national testing, cheap and reliable; in turn this requires a standardized national curriculum. The working out of this quasi-market is said to enhance quality and to restore a flagging competitive ethic throughout education. But there is more: this new governance purports to mask the amount of money spent on education. Here emerges a selective use of league tables: that is, government is quick to publish between-school league tables, but somewhat less than keen to publish between-country league tables which show the percentage of GDP assigned to education in Britain. For example, take the case of expenditure in the United Kingdom (Table 2). In the UK, defence expenditure, as a percentage of GDP, gives it second

Table 2 Expenditure on defence, public safety and education as percentages of GDP, 1998

Country	Defence	Public safety/law & order	Education
Australia	1.9	1.3	3.6
Sweden	2.6	1.5	5.3
UK	3.2	2.0	4.5
New Zealand	1.1	1.5	3.8

Source: OECD (1998b)

place in the OECD. As a nation, the UK is 'fighting' way above its economic weight. It ranks first for expenditure on public safety and law and order, but only ninth for education. So much, therefore, for the economic context which frames contemporary teacher education. But now, let us turn to the second context which frames education: culture.

The cultural context of teacher education

To put it bluntly, within contemporary culture we are witnessing profound uncertainties in relation to each other, in relation to our place of employment, and in our relationship with ourselves as individuals. Let us take these in turn.

First, consider our relationship with others. There is a diminishing level of trust in society. Witness the number of personal alarms, burglar alarms and car alarms which are now being installed. Notice the number of surveillance cameras which pan across the inner city and the shopping malls. The insurance industry is expanding as never before, preying upon our uncertainties. The moral code is said to be fracturing. So-called 'confessional' television programmes all explore the outer limits of convention. Both children and adults are uncertain of the values of the society.

> Morality is privatised, relativistic suspicion becomes the standard response to any talk about moral standards; and it is found uncomfortable, even embarrassing, to discuss morality in public. . . . In fact, this beatification of individual autonomy is a chimera.
> (Dr George Carey, Archbishop of Canterbury, 1997: 3)

Families fracture and reform. We can no longer speak with certainty of the 'family' as an agreed concept, for it now has many permutations.

Political arrangements are changing. Interest groups come and go with the issues of the hour. Increasingly, political factions tend to be concerned with matters of lifestyle – to smoke, or not; to clone or not to; to argue that animals have rights, or not; to go for the full-cholesterol breakfast, or not; and so on. Anthony Giddens tells us that we are *Beyond Left and Right*.

Second, relationships within the workplace are changing. In part this is due to the emergence of post-Fordist modes of management, and in part it is due to the increasing strength of the service sector: the OECD average is 63.7 per cent (OECD, 1998b). More of us in this service sector expend emotional labour, not manual labour. We must give a performance. We must manage our emotions so as to relate to customers and clients. More and more of our identity is made explicit, and recorded by the human resource managers. Post-Fordism requires both a core and a peripheral set of workers. The former are given strong security of tenure; the latter – and they are often women – are required or released in line with the economic cycle. There is a trend towards empowering workers, and to working in groups. Whereas before the worker was controlled by directive or by the technology, now control becomes more invisible, resting deeply in the hidden theories of social scientists. Women are far more likely to have temporary employment, and, when actually working, their hours are more flexible than those of men, on average. In 1996, the percentage of women in employment was 64.2 per cent in the most advanced G7 nations; 57 per cent in the EU-15; and 59.1 per cent in the OECD (OECD, 1998b).

Third, in our relationship to ourselves as individuals there is no more certainty. We live in a consumer society. For some of us, consumerism is a new fundamentalism. How did this state of affairs arise? In the 1960s and 1970s, business sought to widen its product-range. It began to make not just material products but also cultural products. Witness the extent to which culture has been commercialized: sport, religion, tourism, the media, and, waiting in the wings, the biggest prize of all in the commercialization of culture – education. (It is no accident that the solution to some of our educational ills is said to be found in ICT.) As it began to commodify culture, business was able to enlist the advertisers and the media, especially television. Just as obsolescence is built in to material products, so we are encouraged by the media to reflect upon our identity, to become dissatisfied with our image. Thereafter we can redesign it with new symbolizations of ourselves. We are encouraged to change these material and cultural products constantly. Life can become a series of make-overs.

So consumerism confronts us with all manner of choices, and if we choose then we need to reflect upon our identity and what it 'needs'. The advertisers would prefer us to stand before the bathroom mirror each morning and 'reflect', not only upon our physical appearance but also upon our very identity as a person. But this constant reflection can be unsituating, producing existential uncertainty. Melucci puts it thus:

> The search for a safe haven for the self becomes an increasingly critical undertaking, and the individual must build and

continuously rebuild her/his 'home' in the face of the surging flux
of events and relations . . . A world that lives by complexity and
difference cannot escape uncertainty, and it demands from individuals the capacity to change form (the literal meaning).

(Melucci, 1996: 2)

This, argues Melucci (1996: 84), 'has led to the wholesale therapeutiza-
tion of everyday life, so that it now seems more imperative to heal life
than to live it'. These cultural goods symbolize the self. They serve to
generate identities. They make a public statement about the projected
inner selves of those who disport them. Any satisfaction which may
derive from a newly bought identity or therapy is likely to be fleeting:
we are all on short-term contracts with ourselves, in search of meaning.
And, to repeat, science does not provide us with an over-arching world-
view. As we have stated, in some societies magic or religion can perme-
ate all aspects of life, but science cannot. Whilst it has undoubtedly
made great strides in our understanding of the material world, in matters
moral and emotional we are not much further ahead. Melucci again:
'The constitutive dimensions of the self – time and space, health and
sickness, sex and age, birth and death, reproduction and love – are no
longer a datum but a problem' (Melucci, 1996: 2). So, paradoxically,
at a time when we most need those institutions which give us a sense
of security – the welfare state, work, the family, trade unions and
religion – they are less available to us.

Like Melucci, Berman, in his *All That Is Solid Melts Into Air*,
eloquently points up the dilemmas of postmodernism: between a
desire for stability and a desire for new knowledge and experience;
between a search for our roots and our tendency to uproot everything;
between our individualism and our search for national, ethnic and class
identities; between our need for a moral standpoint and a desire to go to
the limit (Berman, 1982: 35). Nor should we expect this state of affairs
to change. The title of Berman's book is based on an extract from the
Communist Manifesto, by Marx (quoted in McLellan, 1977: 224):

Constant revolutionizing of production, uninterrupted disturb-
ance of all social relations, everlasting uncertainty and agitation
distinguish the bourgeois epoch from all earlier times. All fixed,
fast-frozen relationships, with their train of ancient and venerable
prejudices and opinions, are swept away, all new-formed ones
become antiquated before they can ossify. All that is solid melts

into air, all that is holy is profaned, and man [sic] is at last compelled to face with sober senses his real conditions of life, and
his relations with his kind.

What Berman is suggesting is that we should not expect culture to be
other than it is, given the logic of capitalism:

> The one spectre that really haunts the modern ruling class, and
> that really endangers the world it has created in its image, is the
> one thing that traditional elites (and, for that matter, traditional
> masses) have always yearned for: prolonged solid stability. In this
> world, stability can only mean entropy, slow death . . . To say
> that our society is falling apart is only to say that it is alive and
> well.
>
> (Berman, 1982: 95)

It is worth noting how of late notions such as social inclusion have
come to the fore. Ilon (1996: 422), for example, has noted how the
World Bank has shifted from an economic growth focus to a welfare
services focus. Instability caused by profound economic inequalities is
not functional for capitalism.

Consumerism also affects children. Childhood is said by Neil
Postman (1983) to be disappearing. Children are now exposed to
virtually all aspects of adult life. It holds little mystery for them. But
their knowledge of adult life is vicarious – lived through the constructions of the media. Children are left more unsupervised; serial meal-
times are increasingly common. Childhood is also being commodified:
advertisers target children, who will exert 'pester power' over their
parents.

The irony of our present predicament is that neo-liberal economists
have commercialized culture. We are almost required to 'buy into'
consumerism, if we can afford to. And yet now we see the cultural
and political effects of this – flux, fragmentation and uncertainty –
and a desire to regulate the moral order, not only through a national
curriculum for pupils but also – in England – through a compatible
national curriculum for teacher educators. Moreover, these national
curricula will not only serve to regulate the moral order, but will also
be cheaper and efficient: that is to say, the standardization of product
and process is less expensive of time and resources than a plurality of
product and process.

But here we must pause. Not only is society fracturing into consuming individuals who worship in the citadels of consumption. There are
others who lack the money to choose, to buy. They are the so-called
socially excluded, the term for the poor. Here are a few statistics:
twenty per cent of children in the United States live in poverty
(OECD, 1998b); at least one in three children in Scotland, and a
higher proportion of the under-fives, is growing up in households
where income support is the main source of income, giving Scotland
one of the highest child-poverty rates in the European Union (Long
et al., 1996). A fifth of Scottish schoolchildren are entitled to free
school meals. In Glasgow the proportion was 41.4 per cent in 1997–
98 (Scottish Office, 1998). The link between poverty and education
has been established over many years. Similarly, the association
between poverty and health is well established, and was revealed in
very stark terms in Sir Donald Acheson's (1998) *Independent Inquiry
into Inequalities in Health*.

Summary

We have been dealing so far with the economic and cultural contexts
within which teacher education is located. To summarize: the
economic influences upon teacher education are centralizing. That is
to say, the curbs on public expenditure have prompted governments
to spend less on education, and therefore what is spent is subjected to
careful central control. Education – including teacher education – is
ever more regulated. Furthermore, it is standardized, so as to make comparison and competition possible among providers, be they of teacher
education or of schooling. Much-vaunted declarations of choice tend
to apply only to providers, not to the very curriculum which is transmitted. In England, as we have stated, both school education and
teacher education are nationally defined by government or its agencies.
On the other hand, teacher educators and teachers find themselves at
the sharp end of consumer culture. Here the influences of contemporary
culture upon teacher education are very much centrifugal. How does
teacher education prepare teachers to cope with social fragmentation,
a fracturing moral code, consumerism and cultural diversity in all its
forms? In the broader context, diversity is the norm.

So teachers and teacher educators are caught between centralizing
forces and centrifugal forces: the former economic, the latter cultural.
It is little wonder that teachers do not top the poll of satisfied workers.
Gardner and Oswald (1999), in their longitudinal study of job satis-

faction in Britain between 1991 and 1996, note: 'One group of state sector employees is, however, found to have [a] much lower level of job-satisfaction when compared to their counterparts in the government sector, and below that of the private sector. These are teachers' (p. 3). One of the more curious policy decisions by the government in England – as expressed through OFSTED – is to reaffirm so-called whole-class teaching. It is curious because, as the service sector gains more of the share of economic activity, workers will be expected to be team-based, multi-tasking, self-motivated and self-supervising. To this extent, they will be said to be empowered. But how will school-leavers be made ready for this work regime if pedagogy leans towards didacticism? Gee *et al.* (1996), in their influential book *The New Work Order: Behind the Language of the New Capitalism*, set out for us the 'core dilemma of the new capitalism: how to 'control' empowered 'partners' in the absence of visible, overt top-down power. But, they go on, the emerging new cognitive science faces the same dilemma. Here, therefore, is a further instance of Meyer *et al.*'s isomorphism: the social relations of the classroom anticipate those of (some) service-sector work regimes. But this pedagogical style is very expensive, and is difficult to 'engineer'. A government which is bent upon curbing expenditure will tend to drive pedagogical prescriptions to old tried-and-test didactic basics. In the short run this procedure may well save money; in the long term, it may not, because productivity may fall. Here, therefore, we are beginning to touch upon the epistemological basis of teacher education and classroom pedagogy, and how it is influenced not only by financial concerns for efficiency but also by prevailing ideas in both the academy and in the broader culture.

To conclude, we have said that:

- Economic globalization is intensifying competition in the world market. This puts pressure on welfare-state spending, but there is controversy about how much welfare-state spending is optimal for productivity.
- In order to curb expenditure, central governments standardize and rationalize education, not only because it is cheaper but also to enable measures of comparability to be produced for schools and teacher education providers. This enables would-be 'consumers' to choose a provider on the basis of reliable information.
- Whereas economic influences on teacher education will have a centralizing effect, the cultural influences on teacher education will have a centrifugal effect, requiring teacher education to prepare

teachers for cultural diversity and economic inequalities within society.

There is, however, a further influence on teacher education: the academy and the theories which it generates. As we shall see in the next chapter, within the realm of ideas there is no less certainty than there is within the economy and within the culture.

Chapter 3

Philosophical uncertainty and teacher education

This chapter examines the possibility that philosophical approaches to understanding the nature of knowledge might provide the answer to the question, 'What is the knowledge-base that beginning teachers acquire from their teacher education course?' Three possible answers to this question are examined and rejected in favour of a fourth. This last is then defended against a series of possible criticisms and applied to the field of teacher education. The chapter concludes by offering an explanation of the way in which certainty and uncertainty combine to provide an account of the kind of knowledge-base that students encounter on their teacher education courses.

Introduction

We have argued that the economic and cultural contexts within which teacher education operates are typified by uncertainty. Perhaps the intellectual and academic context, the realm of ideas we refer to in the previous chapter, is one that could be seen as providing some sort of fixed and secure framework upon which a clear-cut understanding of teacher education could be built. Such an edifice is built in part on an account of its uniquely identifying knowledge-base. Consequently it is to a consideration of what philosophy, and in particular philosophical approaches to understanding the nature of knowledge, can add to our understanding of the present state of teacher education that we now turn.

The big issue

Something appears to happen to beginning and experienced teachers during their professional development courses. Beginning teachers join their course and, after a period of time, eventually graduate as qualified teachers: experienced teachers take part in professional development courses of various kinds and, after a period of time, eventually graduate with higher degrees as proof that they have successfully completed their course. The obvious question that requires answering is quite what is it that they have experienced on their courses that allows them to graduate successfully? Or, to put the point another way, what is the unique knowledge-base that higher education offers to beginning and experienced teachers on their teacher education courses?

There are at least two reasons why this question should be of significance. The first relates to the notion of whether or not teachers are professionals. It has been argued that:

> the working essentials of education demand that its professionals possess a stock of esoteric knowledge and skills not available to the layman, not to be promiscuously shared with him [sic], and to be conducted within relatively autonomous boundaries.
>
> (Kogan 1989: 136)

The two important points here are, first, that to be recognized as a profession teaching must be able to identify a body of knowledge unique to those practising the profession and, second, that the activity of teaching must be an autonomous one. These two criteria, the epistemological and the social, fit neatly to other forms of public activity that are most commonly identified as professions. Thus those who, for example, practise medicine, nursing, law and civil engineering all clearly have access to complex and abstruse knowledge and, through the medium of their respective professional organizations, have a high degree of autonomy. Admittedly as these professions operate within a democratic society then they are subject to social controls that all organizations operating within such a society accept, so they cannot be fully autonomous (whatever that might mean). All professions therefore are ultimately and properly accountable to the political system that delegates to the individual members of the profession their authority. However, it should be recognized that in most cases that final political power is mediated through the professions' respective councils and not directly from the state to the individual member of the profession. This is the case, for example, currently for teachers in Scotland, and with the recent creation of the General Teaching Council will also apply to teachers in England and Wales.

The social criterion of professionalism, at least before the implementation of recent educational 'reforms' in England and Wales, certainly seemed to apply both to school teaching and to teacher educators. Without appearing to create a mystical golden age or risk drowning in nostalgia it is still possible to recall that only a little while ago teachers, especially primary school teachers, had a great deal of professional autonomy. With the abolition of the external constraints imposed by the eleven-plus examination it was possible to agree with the 1987 Education Secretary that the pre-1988 school curriculum had been 'largely left to individual schools and teachers' (Baker, 1987: 1). This statement fits well with the personal experience of school-teaching of one of the authors, for example, as he can easily remember the problems and pleasures of annually creating a curriculum for the secondary school students he was responsible for, culminating in creating a curriculum and appropriate assessment for Mode 3 CSE, a public examination which gave considerable autonomy to the teachers responsible for offering such courses. The same kind of wide autonomy would apply to the management of schools, subject of course to local authority policies and procedures. In both cases teachers were trusted to make use of their professional expertise so as to operate more or less independently in planning and implementing their own educational policies for the students in their care. In a similar way teacher educators could devise their own curricula for beginning teacher education courses and in-service courses for experienced teachers. With reference to the social criterion at least, teaching was, until recently at least, obviously a profession.

However, given the 'reforms' alluded to earlier, the introduction of the National Curriculum for schoolteachers, a national curriculum for initial teacher education and a form of centralized control of in-service education, all of these being policed by the government's Office for Standards in Education, then the late 1990s have seen what amounts to the removal of virtually all the autonomy that once typified the English teaching profession (see Chapter 5). Even teachers' professional development, and thus the kind of in-service courses that teacher educators in England can create to support the kinds of courses that teachers value for their professional development, are now to be taken out of their hands and identified by the government, as in Figure 1. Thus the social criterion can now no longer be referred to as a means of identifying teachers as professionals. This leaves only the epistemological criterion as a means of justifying the professional status of teachers.

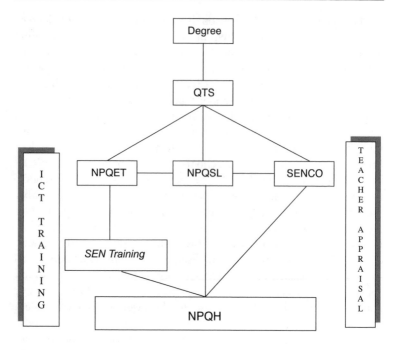

Key

QTS   *Qualified Teacher Status*
NPQET   *National Professional Qualifications for Expert Teachers*
NPQSL   *National Professional Qualification for Subject Leaders*
SENCO   *Special Educational Needs Co-ordinator*
SEN   *Special Educational Needs*
NPQH   *National Professional Qualification for Headship*

Figure 1 Teacher professional development as teacher training (from Gilroy, 1999: 228)

The second reason why it is important to be able to identify the unique contribution of teacher education to educating and developing teachers is that if there is nothing that teacher educators uniquely can contribute to teacher education then the question arises why the government should continue to fund departments of teacher education. Answering the question is not merely a matter of providing a justification for the existence of university departments of teacher education, because if it cannot be answered then there is no reason why virtually anyone could not become a teacher if they so wished. That is, if there is no unique knowledge-base to teacher education then it would seem possible that anyone with a reasonable standard of education could become a teacher without having to waste time and money progressing through a vacuous course for beginning teachers, or developing a non-existent knowledge-base further through equally vacuous in-service courses.

Knowledge and teacher education

Given the central importance of identifying the knowledge-base for teacher education then one might expect it to have been identified some years ago. Unfortunately teacher educators have been strangely reticent in establishing this knowledge-base. Thus a central problem for teacher education in the early 1970s was its 'inability to construct a unified body of knowledge from which educational practice evolves' (Roth, 1972: 9) and even a decade later a similar point was made when it was argued that there was still an 'absence of a universally accepted body of practitioner knowledge' (Watts, 1982: 37). Stones, amongst others, has a clear and as yet uncontested idea of how to identify at least a part of what might be called 'teacher knowledge' (Stones, 1992a), but even the current debate about the identification of teaching competencies does not accept any common assumptions about 'teacher knowledge', to the extent that some would question any form of competency approach (see Whitty, 1993: 270). For McNamara, 'a critical problem facing teachers is that the formal knowledge-base for their professional practice is weak and this enables outsiders to intrude upon their work in the classroom' (McNamara, 1993: 282) in a way that outsiders would not feel capable of intruding, for example, in the professional practice of civil engineering. How, then, might teacher knowledge be defined?

There are at least three approaches to this question which find expression in the field of teacher education, and we will examine each in turn. We will then offer an alternative approach which provides a theoretical and practical basis for our own account of teacher education and which allows for the introduction of new societal demands which impact upon teacher education (see Table 3, page 78).

The objectivist answer

The very question 'What is teacher knowledge?' presupposes an answer that will provide some sort of objective list of knowledge, of the form 'Teacher knowledge is X', where 'X' is a clear-cut list of a knowledge-base similar to the list that, say, a marine engineer might produce when identifying their knowledge-base. Teacher educators would then have a sound base from which to construct the content of a curriculum for teacher education. Such a knowledge-base would be objective in that it was unchanging, a source of certainty, providing a firm foundation for clear-cut unconditional statements about teacher knowledge and the justification for a single and unchanging national curriculum for teacher education.

There have been many attempts by philosophers to identify such objective knowledge. They share a fundamental and ultimately crippling problem, namely how from the non-objective, finite, socially derived world we live in we are able to identify an objective, infinite, cross-cultural knowledge. Thus Plato argued for an objective world of Forms which contained objective knowledge, but was unable to explain how the world we actually inhabit could make reference to it (see especially his *Theatetus*, where he appears to admit this failing). Kant had a similar problem in justifying ethical statements that transcended particular contexts, and the attempts by the epistemologists of the 1960s and 1970s to identify logical and sufficient criteria for the correct use of 'knowledge' (see especially Griffiths, 1967, *passim*) foundered on the impossibility of building a bridge from their formal criteria to the substantial world we live in. A lingering attempt by the once-dominant analytical school of philosophy of education to continue with such empty logical analysis seems to have at last faded away (see Gilroy, 1982).

In teacher education this conception of knowledge, usually implied rather than clearly stated, finds expression in a number of ways. The most obvious can be found in the recent introduction in England of a national curriculum for initial teacher education, which is predicated on the view that there is a clear-cut body of knowledge that all teachers should possess *qua* teachers, coupled to some sort of performance indicators. Indeed the regular inspections of initial teacher education courses by the Office for Standards in Education use a simple mechanistic framework for inspection which produce judgements that are assumed to 'emerge straightforwardly from the objective facts observed by the inspectors', where these judgements 'will themselves be facts which are rendered immune to any polluting effects of interpretation' (Parker, 1997: 19). The sleight of hand whereby an individual's judgement on performance becomes an unquestioned objective 'fact' on a par with, say, the number of students on a course, is breathtaking in its audacity, but none the less flawed for all that. Moreover, this is a point that OFSTED itself once accepted, in stating that 'no subject matter is value neutral, even those which most aspire to objectivity' (OFSTED, 1994, part iv: 18). However, the point that should be noted here, and to which we will return, is that the view that there exists an objective knowledge-base to teacher education has not been, and cannot be, justified. Nevertheless, this view underpins the English central govern-ment's policy decisions regarding teacher education.

The subjectivist answer

The extreme response to the view that knowledge is to be understood in some non-personal, objective, way is to argue that knowledge is created by individuals. Instead of accepting the absolute objectivity of knowl-edge, this viewpoint claims the absolute autonomy of the individual, arguing for the primacy of direct experience as the foundation of all knowledge claims. Thus Russell could argue that 'the meaning you attach to your words must depend on the nature of the objects you are acquainted with' (Russell, 1918: 195), which provides support to his view that 'knowledge by acquaintance' is more fundamental than 'knowledge by description'.

In education this position is reflected in the deschoolers' claims that all knowledge is subjective because:

> We now know that each man [sic] creates his own unique world that he, and he alone, generates whatever reality he can ever know . . . John Donne was wrong. Each man is an island entire of itself . . . Among other things, this means that no man can be absolutely certain of anything.
>
> (Postman and Weingartner, 1969: 100)

The same position can be seen in teacher education by Rowland's assertion that all knowledge is 'my knowledge' (Rowland, 1987: 81).

The fundamental problem that a subjectivist view of knowledge has to face is justifying how it is to be expressed. If all knowledge is, at heart, dependent upon an individual's experience then it follows, with Russell above, that the knowledge of language is also individual-dependent. Thus language would be infinitely ambiguous, a point that Russell (1918: 195) was happy to accept:

> It would be absolutely fatal if people meant the same things by their words. It would make . . . language the most hopeless and useless thing imaginable, because . . . since different people are acquainted with different objects, they would not be able to talk to each other unless they attached quite different meanings to their words.

Yet if Russell were correct then his own argument would require that he could not express that very argument. As he has in fact expressed it then, in the very act of communicating his subjectivist position, he provides a powerful counter-example to his claim that language is infinitely ambiguous.

In teacher education this subjectivist concept of knowledge finds expression in the claims made by those criticizing university-based initial teacher education courses on the grounds that students should be allowed to learn by experience in the classroom how to become a teacher (Lawlor, 1990). Critics of university-based teacher education such as Lawlor would not see themselves as subjectivist, but rather as arguing that there is no knowledge-base for university teacher educators to work from. However, the fact that their alternative depends entirely upon students learning 'on the job', so to speak, clearly assumes that the knowledge-base of teacher education is dependent upon each individual's experience in the classroom. This view is perhaps an inevitable result of teacher educators having difficulty in expressing quite what their unique knowledge-base is, but however it is generated it is clearly subjectivist and suffers from the same incoherence as the subjectivist view of knowledge.

The reflective answer

In the absence of an acceptable objectivist or subjectivist approach to teacher knowledge, teacher educators have seized on Schön's account of professional knowledge as a way of explaining quite what sort of knowledge it is that they are working with. In rejecting what he terms 'technical rationality' on the grounds that it does not allow for the 'ordinary practical knowledge' that his case studies have shown exists in the professions (Schön, 1983: 54) Schön is in effect rejecting objective knowledge. At the same time he is not accepting the chaos of subjectivism (what he calls 'no knowledge at all' – Schön and Rein, 1997: 42), for he wants to argue that professionals work with a tacit form of knowledge which he terms 'knowing-in-action' and which surfaces through a process he terms 'reflection-in-action'. This, then, represents a third response to the question how teacher knowledge might be defined.

Although in many ways Schön's work has come to be the prevailing orthodoxy in teacher education, this alternative account of knowledge has begun to be criticized (see for example Newman, 1999). The criticism takes two forms. The first is that Schön's argument that the positing of tacit knowledge resolves Plato's Meno paradox (of how we come to know something that we do not know we know) is suspect, as the paradox is by definition irresolvable (Gilroy, 1993: 129–31). The second is that there is no need to tie oneself in reflective knots so as to create a new theory of knowledge to explain the nature of professional education, as there already exists a theory of knowledge that can accommodate the 'situations of uncertainty and uniqueness' (Schön, 1983: 61) which Schön claims typify professional practice.

Those who wish to relate Schön's work to teacher education have to be able to show how the Meno paradox relates to the situation beginning or experienced teachers and their teacher educators find themselves in. For example, Meno's slave is placed in a situation where he would appear incapable of recognizing what he is supposed to be learning as he has never had acquaintance with the knowledge he supposedly reveals, hence the notion of a paradox that Schön plays on. However, neither beginning nor experienced teachers are in this position. Even beginning teachers already possess 'powerful imitative and intuitive understandings of what teaching is' (Squirrell et al., 1990: 72), based on the variety of teaching situations they have experienced as students. It is therefore unclear how an appeal to knowing-in-action, utilizing a technique of reflection-in-action, and designed to resolve a paradox concerning the nature of professional knowledge, could apply to a situation where that paradox does not exist.

The contextualist answer

In examining the objectivist approach to knowledge it was claimed that such a view of knowledge had to give an explanation of how it is possible to have absolutely certain knowledge through a medium provided by the apparently uncertain world that we live in. One philosopher, Wittgenstein, writing in the early part of the twentieth century, claimed that this was possible through the medium of a certain kind of logical syntax to 'avoid ambiguity' (Wittgenstein, 1921: 3.325) because 'outside logic everything is accidental', but inside logic we have access to law-like necessities (1921: 6.3) through what he termed elementary propositions, which in some sense picture reality. Unfortunately, as Wittgenstein himself accepted, it is not possible to give even a single example of an elementary proposition on this account of knowledge because to do so one would have to make use of ordinary language which, by definition, is not the pure language of logic. Thus this position has the same difficulty alluded to earlier that infects any objectivist account of knowledge.

However, Wittgenstein came to see that he had misunderstood the way in which language operates, perhaps in part because of his growing interest in anthropology (Wittgenstein, 1930). He criticized his early objectivist account, arguing that there is no need to improve on ordinary language by inventing 'an ideal language' (Wittgenstein, 1933: 28) and that logic's 'simple and rigid rules' were an inappropriate way of making sense of language's variety of meanings (1993: 83). He explicitly abandoned the search for certainty, arguing that it is the social system we operate in that provides the criteria against which we judge whether something is perceived as being knowledge or falsehood (Wittgenstein, 1949: §108, 194). These criteria are not logical rules, but are social conventions reflecting the customs of a particular community, these customs providing the medium within which language operates. As with a game it is quite possible to operate in accord with linguistic rules 'without ever learning or formulating them', by being bound by the social purpose of that particular language-game (Wittgenstein, 1933: §31, §87). Finally, an individual can show that they understand the criteria for a particular aspect of knowledge through their actual use of the criterion, so there would be what might be called a certainty of the moment (otherwise language would have no meaning), but this certainty is only fixed at that time for that social group and is not immutable. Thus philosophy consists not of some sort of linguistic analysis which relates language to some ideal certain world of *logic*, but rather of describing and illuminating in rigorous ways how language variously operates in messy and uncertain social *contexts* (Wittgenstein, 1953: §109). In an important sense this moves philosophy from arid linguistic analysis towards a form of sociolinguistic anthropology, where the philosopher *qua* anthropologist studies the social contexts which provide meaning to language (compare Chapter 5, p. 88). There have been a number of terms advanced for this approach to philosophy (such as functional analysis, cluster analysis and criterial semantics), but the emphasis on describing and critically illuminating the contexts

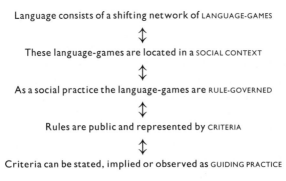

Language consists of a shifting network of LANGUAGE-GAMES

↕

These language-games are located in a SOCIAL CONTEXT

↕

As a social practice the language-games are RULE-GOVERNED

↕

Rules are public and represented by CRITERIA

↕

Criteria can be stated, implied or observed as GUIDING PRACTICE

Figure 2 Concepts in contextualism

within which practice operates so as to identify the rules that underpin that practice suggests the term 'contextualism' opted for here.

This account of Wittgenstein's philosophy, of course, does scant justice to the complexities of his work, which has been examined in detail elsewhere (Gilroy, 1996: chapter 8 *passim*). However, what should be clear is that there are a number of key interconnected concepts in contextualism, as in Figure 2. There are a number of ways in which contextualism relates to teacher education. One would be that the implication in the question 'What is teacher knowledge?' that there is a simple and definite answer to the question needs addressing. There is no simple checklist of teacher knowledge, in the same way as there is no all-embracing checklist to identify what counts as knowledge. Instead, the practice of teaching reveals interconnected sets of rule-governed behaviour which vary from social context to context. It is possible to identify some of these rules, but it would be a basic mistake to attempt to generalize from them so as to produce a definitive list of teacher knowledge, as such a generalization would require every school, every student and every teacher to be operating with the same criteria governing their behaviour.

Another way in which contextualism relates to teacher education is to pick up on the criticism levelled earlier against those using Schön's work to identify teacher knowledge, namely that student teachers are not in the same position as Meno's slave, in that they already possess an understanding of what counts as teaching. If teacher knowledge is indeed represented by different forms of socialization, then student teachers are resocialized as they come to reconceptualize what they understand teaching to be. This is not to be achieved simply by placing them in front of a classroom of children, or by describing the process of teaching from the safety of the university education department. The rule-governed nature of the 'game' of teaching requires first practice and second the understanding of the criteria that guide this practice, which would include experiencing and grasping the shifting and varied nature of the criteria guiding their practice. It is the first of these requirements that student teachers naturally concentrate on as they work at surviving in the classroom, but it is the second that would allow them to begin to see the ways in which their practice is rule-governed, connected to a social context and thus subject to change.

Contextualism attacked

There are certain terms that any academic uses with particular care. For example, it has been claimed that it is unwise to talk about the aims of education, as to do so is to fall into the open jaws of philosophers of education. A similar warning might well be used with reference to the term 'relativism'. When such a philosophical position is castigated as 'the abyss of relativism' (Martin, 1976: 20), as 'the foul pit of relativism' (Bloor, 1976: 142) and as being 'incoherent' (Vallicella, 1984: 463) or 'rearing its ugly head' (Weinert, 1984: 376), then it is natural to tread warily so as to avoid the odium in which the position is held by some. Indeed, given the claim that a relativist position leads to a 'do-nothing policy of educational practice' (Martin, 1976) then any educationist might well turn their back on such a position.

There are at least two confusions that can be made when referring to relativism. The first is in thinking that it is some form of hidden subjectivism, arguing that knowledge is to be located only in the individual; the second in thinking that it is some form of disguised objectivism, appealing surreptitiously to an objective account of knowledge. A third problem is that in stating that all knowledge is relative the relativist is at one and the same time offering an example of non-relative knowledge, and it is this problem of reflexivity which has led to the claim that relativism 'can neither be stated coherently nor held consistently' (Trigg, 1976: 220).

It is obvious that identifying oneself as a relativist is fraught with difficulties. Moreover, the contextualism introduced in this chapter (where the interconnected concepts of language-games operating in a social context, governed by rules which are identified as criteria guiding social practice, replace the flawed objectivist account of knowledge) would at first sight appear to be a form of relativism. If there are, as there clearly are, differing social contexts, then there would seem to be different criteria for identifying knowledge and so knowledge would seem to be relative. Thus this argument would seem to allow for a rampant relativism, as not only knowledge but ethics, metaphysics and language-meaning itself would all seem to be relative to particular social contexts. As there are a potentially infinite number of social contexts then there would be an infinite number of accounts of knowledge, ethics, world-views and language-meanings. It would be hard to distinguish between this account and that of a purely subjectivist one and, given its emphasis on the social context, it could perhaps be described as 'social solipsism' (Lukes, 1974: 160). More recently it has been described as 'magical antirealism . . . [which] holds that the mind creates objects' (Carter and Bahde, 1998: 318). As such it would be as incoherent as any subjectivist account of knowledge and of little or no use for coming to an understanding of social and cultural phenomena. It would seem that one is driven back to some objectivist account of knowledge. What then of knowledge in the New Age of uncertainty?

Contextualism defended

It may well be that simplistic forms of cultural relativism lead inevitably to the incoherence of subjectivism, a point well made by Flew in his criticism of what he terms 'social idealism' as evidenced in certain approaches to the sociology of knowledge (Flew, 1976: 12). If contextualism is to be identified as some form of relativism (see for example Trigg, 1973: 31 and Gellner, 1974: 20) then clearly the way in which it avoids the problems identified above needs to be established.

This section of the book will therefore represent a defence of contextualism against the charge of being an extreme form of relativism. In doing this we will be arguing that its critics have not properly understood the subtleties of the position and, moreover, that once one accepts the position then one is provided with a tool with which to make sense of various tensions and strains in teacher education.

Argument by dichotomy: the third way

As with much that exercises the minds of western thinkers, philosophical relativism can be traced back to the classical Greek thinkers as they wrestled with the problem of explaining how it was possible to have objective, fixed and certain knowledge in what appeared to be a non-objective, unstable and uncertain world. Thus pre-Socratics such as Parmenides and Zeno took considerable delight in creating linguistic paradoxes which purported to show that the knowledge we appeared to derive from our sensory apparatus was in fact unsound. It was this tradition, coupled to the sophistic notion that 'all appearances are equally true' (Kerferd, 1981: 72), that middle-period Plato was reacting against when he created his objective world of Forms. The problem was nicely caught by Sextus, who claimed that 'we must suspend judgment about the nature of objects' because we have no way independent of our own nature with which to access objects (Annas and Barnes, 1985: 129).

Flowing from this traditional exposition of the central philosophical problem of knowledge is the assumption that we can operate only with argument by dichotomy. This mode of argument takes the form of identifying two polar opposites and then trying to find a third way which somehow avoids the weaknesses of both. For example, if in trying to understand the nature of knowledge one has to choose only between an objective or a subjective account then it is perhaps not surprising that there should be the sorts of difficulties identified above with objectivist and subjectivist accounts of professional knowledge. Indeed, Schön's reflective practitioner account that seems at the moment to have the most currency in teacher education can be seen as operating along these lines, positing a straightforward dichotomy between what he terms the dominant technical-rationalist 'positivist epistemology of practice' (Schön, 1983: 48) and an account of knowledge, an epistemology, which is more subjective or tacit.

Schön, of course, bridges the dichotomy by arguing for what he identifies as a new 'epistemology of practice' (1983: 113), knowing-in-action, which somehow allows for both the objective and subjective elements of professional knowledge to be identified without at the same time being either objectivist or subjectivist. This account has been criticized above, but is here offered as an example of a modern argument by dichotomy which, as such, can be 'too neat, too clean – and quite misleading' (Shulman, 1988: 33). Another example of such a form of argument can be seen in aspects of the modernist/postmodernist debate that also appears to suffer from the same problem of arguing from dichotomies, even though 'postmodernism [is] supposedly hostile to binary oppositions' (Eagleton, 2000: 92), with some at least (see Barrow, 1997: 73–5), appearing to share Schön's problem of offering 'an either-or description of a situation that is actually a both-and'

(Fenstermacher, 1988: 33). It is this notion of the 'both-and' which we now wish to examine in relation to contextualism and professional knowledge so as to substantiate the claim made earlier that contextualism can provide a useful foundation from which both to understand the current situation teacher education finds itself in and to develop that understanding further. To do this we will need to turn to arguments concerning the objective, or otherwise, status of scientific knowledge.

Contextualism as 'both-and', not 'either-or'

The philosophical arguments about the nature of knowledge have spilled over into the philosophy of science, with clear parallels between the two sets of arguments. The obvious counter-example to any vaguely relativistic account of knowledge would be that of scientific knowledge. It is here, if nowhere else, that objective, fixed and certain knowledge seems to lie and it is here, of course, that the postmodernists identify modernity *par excellence*, for it is here that there seems to be a 'priority of *the world* over *our descriptions* of the world' (Parker, 1997: 25). It is also here that there seems to be an outbreak of argument by dichotomy.

The objectivist approach to scientific knowledge, echoing that of the philosophical objectivist, is well described by Chalmers as being 'derived in some rigorous way from the facts of experience acquired by observation and experiment . . . Scientific knowledge is reliable knowledge because it is objectively proven knowledge' (Chalmers, 1978: 1). He continues by establishing that the three assumptions that this account relies on, the notion of pure observation, of science proceeding by accumulating confirmations of hypotheses, and of the validity of induction, are at best suspect and at worst simply false. There have been a number of different ways of criticizing this account and offering an alternative, and at least one of these is seen as being relativist.

The possibly relativist account is that offered by Kuhn. In claiming that science develops by means of 'scientific revolutions' (Kuhn, 1970: 92), whereby communities of scientists committed to one paradigmatic approach to their subject lose their confidence in that particular approach, Kuhn argues that 'the differences between successive paradigms are both necessary and irreconcilable' (1970: 103). It would seem to follow that what counts as acceptable scientific knowledge is dependent upon which scientific community, or paradigm, one owes allegiance to. Interpreted in this way Kuhn's work is clearly a relativistic thesis, with knowledge being group-dependent. It is also possible to generate some sort of subjectivism from the thesis, for there are no objective standards of rationality to appeal to when judging between competing paradigms, only standards created by the paradigms themselves. In this way Kuhn's account of the development and progress of scientific knowledge could be seen as an example of Lukes's social solipsism alluded to above, where the subjectivity of the group replaces that of the individual.

A third account of scientific knowledge is that of Popper. Popper's claim to have resolved the problem of induction (Popper, 1971: 1), coupled to his acceptance of the fact that observations are not 'pure', leads naturally to his well-known account of science as being identified by the criterion of falsification. This in turn led him to examine in more detail the nature of knowledge and to claim that 'There is no absolute certainty, though enough certainty for practical purposes. The quest for certainty, for a secure basis of knowledge, has to be abandoned' (Popper, 1972: 37). Despite the apparent abandonment of absolute certainty Popper, in criticizing Kuhn's apparently relativistic account of scientific knowledge as proceeding by means of competing paradigms (Kuhn, 1970), took great pains to distinguish his position from that of relativism. For example, he says, 'I do believe in "absolute" or "objective" truth' (Popper, 1970: 56) and he also argued that through attempting to falsify beliefs we can 'approach nearer to the truth' (Popper, 1963: 248). What then can be made of a position which seems to be both denying and accepting objectivity?

It is at this point that we would wish to reintroduce the contextualism argued for earlier, for it is here that the subtlety of that position becomes clear. In the same way as Popper appears to be both accepting and rejecting objectivity so contextualism seems caught in the same contradiction. We now need to explain how it is possible to be both an objectivist (of sorts) and a relativist (of sorts): in doing so it is necessary to make use of the 'both-and' approach to a complex situation, as opposed to the dichotomous 'either-or'.

What has to be avoided is both a context-free (transcendental) argument for objectivity and a context-bound (socially subjective) argument for the relativity of knowledge. By arguing that knowledge claims are to be located within language-games which have their life within various social contexts, one avoids any attempt at some sort of supra-objectivity, only a straightforward description of how knowledge is to be found in practice. By arguing that language-games are governed by rules provided by criteria, one avoids any attempt at accepting that 'anything goes' for knowledge. Within a set of language-games there are

Figure 3 Lakatos and scientific research programmes

certain limited and temporary objectivities, in that, without the base of some sort of agreement on criteria for the operation of the game's rules, the game itself could not be played. In this way it is possible to accept the Popperian notion of 'certainty for practical purposes' without at the same time being either an objectivist or a subjectivist.

To return to the philosophy of science for a moment. Lakatos's conception of scientific research programmes as consisting of a 'hard core', a protective belt of additional assumptions and external hypotheses (see Figure 3), nicely captures the subtlety of Popper's account of knowledge and our explanation of contextualism. It is the hard core which uniquely identifies a research programme and which is irrefutable 'by the methodological decision of its protagonists' (Lakatos, 1970: 133): similarly, it is particular social contexts allied to their practices, within which language-games can be located, that represents the 'given' for a contextualist. Lakatos's protective belts of assumptions and hypotheses are the point at which tests (through confirmation or falsification) take place: similarly, it is through an examination of a language-game's rules and their criteria that a language-game, and thus its social context, can, for a contextualist, develop and change, as the assumptions underpinning a particular social context are interpreted and critically analysed. However, one significant addition we would make to Figure 3 is the view that in any complex, pluralistic, society there is inevitably more than one 'hard core' and therefore a plurality of 'additional assumptions' and 'hypotheses' surrounding them and, indeed, intertwining one set with another. It is therefore an important social skill in such societies to be able to move easily from one set of knowledge-bases to another, made that much more difficult when the bases are tacit. This requires a skill which teachers and teacher educators are necessarily involved with passing on, the more so if the taken-for-granted assumptions that provide the context, the 'hard core', of their society are constantly changing.

In passing it is worth noting that attempts to reconstruct the knowledge-base of teacher education, by accelerating the move away from the grand narratives of the disciplines to niche narratives provided through personal histories presented as reflective practice (see Chapter 4: 77ff), would represent a double fallacy. The first is connected to the insidious assumption that one has to choose between two alternatives, the 'either-or' fallacy, where either the disciplines or reflective practice can on their own provide the single knowledge-base to teacher education. The second is to assume that the context within which teacher education operates is a simple one so that there is a single answer to the question, 'What is teacher knowledge?' If we take the contextualist approach argued for here, it becomes possible to see that there are different kinds of knowledge involved and that the two narrative forms mentioned above are not mutually exclusive, so allowing for a 'both-and' account to illuminating teacher knowledge (see below). That is to say, there are a number of different approaches to accessing the hard core, the additional assumptions and the hypotheses that identify a particular aspect of the theory and practice of education. These are mutually *inclusive* rather than mutually *exclusive*. This inclusivity is absolutely necessary, given the fact that what is recognized as the hard core, additional assumptions and hypotheses, is more often than not *itself* the subject of argument (with our book being an example of precisely this sort of fundamental disagreement with current understanding of the field of teacher education).

Contextualism in action

We would argue that contextualism avoids the criticisms levelled against relativism whilst at the same time explaining how it is possible to identify both certainty and uncertainty within its account of knowledge. It does this in part by describing as accurately as possible the way in which language operates and in part by refusing to operate with constraining dichotomies. How can it be used to navigate through some of the key features of the current landscape of teacher education?

Schön's reflective practice

This position has already been examined and identified as having a number of significant problems. However, from a contextualist's standpoint there is no need for Schön to posit a new form of knowledge, 'knowledge-in-action', with its attendant epistemological complexities, to attempt to explain the knowledge-base from which professionals work. Leaving aside the damaging ambiguities inherent in the notion of reflective practice (see Gilroy, 1993), the contextualist can easily accommodate Schön's case studies by showing that in effect what happens when the expert works with novices is a convergence of meaning, in effect a sharing of the implicit and explicit rules that govern the hard core of the social practice under consideration (see especially Newman, 1999: 148ff). It is not that some sort of objective knowledge (the technical-rational) is passed on in an overt way: rather, it is through activities such as shaping, example and immersion into the particular context, followed by a critical illumination of that activity's context, that the novice comes to share the rules and absorb a technical vocabulary that provide the structure for that particular language-game's activities and which allows them to go below the taken-for-granted assumptions with which teachers operate (see also Chapter 4: 76ff). They unknowingly enter, so to speak, the hard core of that community through using its language-games, the hypotheses and overt assumptions that protect the covert assumptions of that community. In this way the problems inherent in the concept of *reflective* practice are resolved by reinterpreting the rich case studies that Schön provides as, in effect, *contextualist* practices.

Modernism, postmodernism and contextualism

This chapter has so far studiously avoided any extended reference to the modernist/postmodernist debate within teacher education. It seemed best to establish contextualism and its connection to teacher education first before making connections to the other central themes of this book. However, it should be clear that there are echoes of the modernist/postmodernist debate in what has so far been developed, as the following two examples make clear.

The first example comes from recognizing that a key feature of the postmodernist position is its approach to the notion of Truth. Usher and Edwards in discussing Lacan's work make the point that 'the truth can never be fully and finally spoken' (Usher and Edwards,

1994: 73) and yet later quote with approval Foucault's assertion that 'each society has its regime of truth' (Foucault, 1980: 131, cited in Usher and Edwards, 1994: 87). What we seem to have here is another example of the either/or, of the dichotomous argument that there is either certain Truth or uncertain truths, compounded by the problem of reflexivity, in that by stating that there is no such thing as certain Truth then one appears to have produced an example of certain Truth (cf. Barrow, 1997: 75). A variation of this criticism can be seen in Bridges's recent analysis of Stronach and MacLure's postmodernist approach to educational research, where he argues that Stronach and MacLure are making use of the very concepts of rationality they claim to be critiquing (Bridges, 1999: 612–15).

For a contextualist the notion of truth is very much one of coherence, but of coherence with the hard core of assumptions that identify the particular community that is under discussion. In this way one can speak of different contexts within which the concept of truth is operating. For example, the community under consideration will be making use of their understanding of truth, as evidenced in their practice and the criteria governing that practice, whilst another might be examining that community's particular language-games to see how they connect to the group's purposes. The danger of such philosophical anthropology, of course, is in trying to use one conception of truth to understand the application of another, and so ignoring the contextualist argument that radically different language-games regarding truth are 'incorrigible if viewed from the inside and corrigible if viewed from the outside' (Körner, 1974: 14). Thus when Hartley argues that at present 'the cultural code and the economic code are at odds' (Hartley, 1997: 151) he is pointing to two descriptions of what might once have been seen as the same phenomenon, modern society, and arguing that 'education policy has sought to merge the cultural and economic codes' (1997: 153). Attempts to enforce that merger are, for a contextualist, suspect in that one description or interpretation of a phenomenon is being offered as if it were the only acceptable description. This represents an attempted domination by political assertion which has in fact been more or less successful, in England at least.

On this view the postmodernists can be seen either as trying to use a different language-game to that which dominated modernity's academic discourse or as offering an alternative perspective on that discourse. The first approach can be judged only against its own criteria and rules, the second by the power of its description. However, for a contextualist it would be a fundamental error to judge either by the rules of another linguistic community and also to assume that these two approaches are mutually exclusive (for in offering an alternative perspective on the discourse of modernity the postmoderns are inevitably led into an alternative form of modernism).

To put this point another way, the postmodernists could be interpreted as bursting through the accepted hypotheses and protective assumptions of the modernist community and attempting to reinterpret their hard core directly. It is for this reason that their work is at times confusing (and perhaps confused), for the criteria whereby confusion is normally to be identified are themselves under attack. Interpretation of positions such as modernism or postmodernism is a necessary part of a description of such positions and which criteria to use, which language-game's rules, to identify the failure or success of a description is itself subject to debate (see most recently Hager and Peters, 2000: 309ff).

A second way in which contextualism can be used to make sense of the modernist/postmodernist debate is by observing that if modernism is to be typified by appeals to certainty then key philosophical terms such as positivism, objectivism, linguistic analysis and technical rationality are clearly in the modernist tradition. Forms of teacher education that are connected to such philosophical viewpoints can thus be seen as modernist. Indeed, one of the contradictions that teacher education in particular has to deal with is that it would appear to be locked into a modernist approach, or what Foucault termed an 'attitude' (Foucault, 1984: 39), whilst operating within a postmodernist milieu. With Usher and Edwards:

> Educational theory and practice is founded on the discourse of modernity and its self-understandings have been forged by that discourse's basic and implicit assumptions . . . The very rationale of the educational process and the role of the educator is founded on modernity's self-motivated, self-directing, rational subject, capable of exercising individual agency.
>
> (Usher and Edwards, 1994: 2)

However, the contextualist account offered here suggests links with postmodernity, links that are made explicit by Lyotard. Thus Wittgenstein's rejection of the search for certainty is echoed by Lyotard's definition of the postmodern as 'incredulity toward metanarratives' (Lyotard, 1979: xxiv) and clearly, as Peters has argued, Lyotard 'has assimilated the Wittgensteinian understanding of language-games' (Peters, 1995: 391). A more tentative connection can be derived from the fact that as early as 1930 Wittgenstein was writing about cultural anthropology, a major source for the development of postmodern thought, arguing that explanations of radically different social practices can result only in alternative descriptions of those practices, rather than establishing that one set of practices is in some sense superior to another (Wittgenstein, 1930: 61–3).

It could be argued that philosophy can lend support to current forms of teacher education only if it is perceived as a modernist, non-contextualist, enterprise. The current centralization of a monistic form of teacher education in England and Wales, in particular the National Curriculum for teacher education, the policing of that curriculum by the Office for Standards in Education and the implication that there is a straightforward knowledge-base that can be taught by teacher educators, policed by ever-increasing quality audits, is clearly all part of a modernist tradition.

However, this approach to knowledge is obviously one that is based on a notion of power. As has been shown, a contextualist would argue that there is nothing coherent in either an objectivist or subjectivist account of knowledge and, consequently, the current situation regarding teacher education and teacher knowledge is one that requires a contextualist critique. That critique would point to the fact that merely enforcing a particular account of teacher knowledge and the teacher education system it requires does no more than assert that one form of teacher knowledge is the only form of knowledge, 'justifying' the unjustifiable through the raw exercise of power. Contextualism's acceptance of the essential fluidity of knowledge is thus a philosophy that argues against the very certainties that the current form of teacher education relies upon (see Chapter 5: 85ff). If philosophy cannot provide a sound objectivist epistemological foundation for teacher education, perhaps one of the other major intellectual disciplines can and it is these which we will examine next. Of course, a possible alternative would be to accept that, as argued for in this chapter, it is not possible to find an objectivist knowledge-base for teacher education and to recognize that the one that is currently policed in England by OFSTED is a fiction enforced by political fiat.

Contextualism and teacher education

It has already been argued that contextualist approaches to knowledge imply that there is no one set of knowledge which would identify the professional knowledge of teachers. Consequently there would appear to be no obvious knowledge-base for teacher educators to transmit to their students. Yet in England at least there now exists a national curriculum for teacher education, supported by an audit culture to ensure that the curriculum is in fact delivered, which suggests that some at least feel that they can dictate what that knowledge-base is.

At this point we appear to have hit upon what might be termed the legal hard core knowledge-base. By that we mean it is something both identified and policed by the central government, policed of course by the Office for Standards in Education as it enforces the domination of one description of the curriculum over another. But for a contextualist this is merely one amongst many epistemological programmes, one amongst many social communities of practice, which teachers and teacher educators step into and out of as necessity demands. Thus when OFSTED arrives to inspect or police schools and teacher education institutions the many public criticisms of their approach (not least the use of highly subjective criteria to make what are claimed to be objective judgements – see Gilroy and Wilcox, 1997) are set aside whilst teachers and teacher educators play the language-game being forced upon them.

In addition to the legal epistemological core there also appear to be others linked to the particular social contexts of educational institutions, which in turn find expression through the activities of that community, and which the agents of the official core cannot easily stamp out. The reason for their failure is that the actual practical situations that teachers and teacher educators find themselves in are so pressing, varied and uncertain that, like it or not, such professionals have to make use of a contextualist approach to knowledge. The immediate professional responses to the demands of a practical situation create limited certainties which guide practice they are not something that can be dictated from afar. It is this ability to adapt to a series of limited certainties which best identifies the teacher professional and which teacher educators attempt to inculcate and model, as they themselves play a multitude of language-games.

This said it is interesting to compare two studies of teacher education in Europe. The first talked about broad trends being 'detectable in most member states of the European Union' (Buchberger and Beernaert, 1995: 398) and argued that 'It is debatable whether (prospective) teachers may acquire problem solving capacity in those models of ITE which focus on the transmission of knowledge products or on recipes for practice' (402). A mere four years on and the second study addresses this issue directly, claiming that static conceptions of teacher education have the hidden assumptions that initial teacher education has the ability to:

> equip prospective teachers with all those competencies that seem to be necessary to competently fulfil the tasks of the teaching profession over a life-long career, and at the same time to develop the problem-solving capacity necessary to meet rapidly changing tasks of teaching and the teaching profession.
>
> While these assumptions may, to some extent, have been valid in static societies, they are inappropriate in the dynamic and rapidly changing contexts of the today.
>
> (Buchberger *et al.*, 2000: 17)

It can be seen that the first study's description of a relatively stable system across Europe has been replaced with one that accepts the notion of fluidity. Moreover, although not citing Hartley, the second study describes a similar scenario to his, whereby the state attempts to control teacher education through various forms of 'increasing economic rationality' (2000: 32–3). Thus, even at the very general level of European provision for teacher education, it can be seen that the paradox of requiring that teacher education should be involved with providing students with the skills necessary to operate in an essentially uncertain medium, but through a centrally dictated and policed curriculum, is left unresolved. However, what should be clear from this chapter is that modern philosophy's approach to understanding the nature of knowledge cannot be used to lend even a superficial respectability to a policy which is at heart no more than some form of unjustifiable and crude political manipulation of teacher education. It is to the political – and thus policy – solutions to the problems they perceive in teacher education that we now turn.

Chapter 4

Modernist policy solutions

Since 1979 in Britain, and more latterly in other countries, the professions within the welfare state have had to do more with less. In some countries teachers have been blamed for a lack of economic competitiveness with the emergent Pacific-rim economies, and international league-table data on standards of mathematics and science have underlined what is seen as an under-performance by the more traditional capitalist economies. Reviews of teacher education by central governments (as in England and Wales), by the profession itself (the Holmes Group reports), or by independent think-tanks, have all caught teacher education in their gaze. Back-to-basics and what-works solutions have been imposed by some governments. These solutions have sought to render certain the uncertainties which were dealt with in Chapter 2. Examples are drawn from England, Wales and the United States.

Teacher education: some modernist approaches

This chapter considers so-called modernist attempts to deal with teacher education since the 1960s. First, however, it is necessary to revisit the term 'modernity', and to distinguish it from the premodern – that is, from the medieval. Toulmin sets out the shift in our modes of thought from the beginning of the seventeenth century:

> In a dozen areas, the modes of life and thought in modern Europe from 1700 on (modern science and medicine, engineering and institutions) were assumed to be more rational than those typical of medieval Europe, or those found in less developed societies and cultures today. Further, it was assumed that uniquely rational procedures exist for handling the intellectual and practical problems of any field of study, processes which are available to anyone

who sets superstition and mythology aside, and attacks those problems in ways free of local prejudice and transient fashion.

(Toulmin, 1990: 11)

For Toulmin, modernity rests on three pillars: first, *certainty*; second, *formal rationality* (or *systematicity*); and third, the *clean slate* (Toulmin, 1990: 179). *Certainty* implies that, through theory and empirical research, we can come to understand the world; and, having understood it, we can then change it for the better. Thus it is that progress is said to be possible. Science gives us faith in the future. No longer shall we fall victim to the gurus and to the magicians. *Formal rationality* means the application of rules, laws and regulations to more and more aspects of our lives, thereby entrapping us in what Max Weber calls the 'iron cage of bureaucratic rationality'. But this formal rationality has the effect of disenchanting us – that is, of suppressing our affects. For example, in many service-sector jobs, workers must manage their emotions for a performative purpose. The expressive is instrumentalized. In forging an emotional (and therefore profitable) bond between the client and the worker, the latter may express 'emotions' which are insincere, yet necessary for the effective discharge of their duties. Toulmin's third pillar of modernity, the *clean slate*, means that somehow, in the modern way, we can set aside history and culture, and cast ourselves anew. Notice, for example, the widespread use of the prefix *re-* in contemporary life. But, argues Toulmin, this attempt to wipe the slate clean is illusory: 'We are not compelled to choose between 16th-century humanism and 17th-century exact science; rather, we need to hang on to the positive achievements of them both' (Toulmin, 1990: 181). For Toulmin, the three-pillar model of modernity has served its purpose: it has reached its limits:

This model served constructive ends in the 17th century, but the rigidity it imposed on rational practice in a world of independent and separate agents is no longer appropriate in the late 20th century, which is a time of increasing interdependence, cultural diversity and historical change . . . By continuing to impose on thought and action all the demands of unreconstructed Modernity – rigor, exactitude, and system – we risk making our ideas and institutions not just stable but sclerotic, and being unable to modify them in reasonable ways to meet the fresh demands of novel situations.

(Toulmin, 1990: 184)

Science, he argues, must be applied for the good of humanity. Facts cannot be divorced from values. Modernity must be humanized, thereby connecting modernity to premodernity; the head with the heart, reason with emotion. Nor, after Habermas, should the democratizing efforts of modernity be underestimated, or renounced. In his own commentary on modernity, Berman (1982: 86) anticipated Toulmin's concern: our quest should be 'to create new modes of modernity, in which man will not exist for the sake of development, but development for the sake of man'. Before our discussion of modernist solutions to teacher education, we would do well to remind ourselves of the profound shifts that have occurred since the 1960s. Toulmin again:

> After the turbulence of the 1960s and '70s, the decade of the '80s was a time for nostalgia rather than imagination. From the 1960s on, in many countries, too much social stress developed too quickly: notably, the unresolved conflicts left over from the Vietnam War, and the rapid economic changes arising from the automation of industry, the growing service economy, and international competition. The modern dream of an order of sovereign 'nations' again became attractive, and nostalgia led people to revive their pride in nationhood, and to do as little as possible to upset the nation-state system.
>
> (Toulmin, 1990: 205)

We argued earlier that there are conflicting forces acting on education. First, there are centralizing forces which derive in part from increasing international competition. This requires nation states to invoke 'best value', 'more-for-less' approaches to their management of the welfare state. This quest for efficiency begets standardization. Standardization itself implies that the hand of central government must fall firmly on the shoulder of educational institutions, curbing variety so as to facilitate the generation of objective measures of performance. Here, therefore, are centripetal forces at work on education. Second, in contrast, there are forces on education which stress difference, diversity and inequality. This centrifugal flux and uncertainty are nevertheless functional for business because it must renew the demand for its goods and services. Moreover, these two sets of forces intersect. Turbulence and stresses are revealed. Indeed the very discourse of education finds seemingly contradictory registers of terms being interwoven: choice and control; national standards and devolved management; reflection and direction. Thus it is that contemporary policy-makers seem to lead us through a dance of the dialectic.

In this chapter we focus upon a number of recent and contemporary attempts to reconcile these contradictions which act upon teacher education. In order to help us to structure our thinking about these policies, we shall deal with them according to a number of headings. These are:

(a) The locus of control: that is to say, who defines what shall count as teacher education? Is it government, whether central or local; the profession and its constituent bodies; the academy; the market; or some combination of these?

(b) The content of teacher education: that is to say, what shall comprise teacher education? More specifically,

(i) Is this content seen to be universalistic and generic? There are two ways of thinking about this:

First, can we speak of a knowledge-base for teacher education which rests firmly upon the foundation of public theory which has been generated in the universities?

Second, is this content seen to be generic, but yet detached from any theoretical underpinning? Put another way: are there rule-of-thumb tips for teachers which are said to constitute best practice? Here, evidence-based practice would mean one which was not theory-driven, but distilled from a meta-analysis of observed practice.

(ii) Or does this content purport to be theoretically based, but yet does not have general application? This implies a contradiction, for our notion of theory implies that it is universal, not local; and, equally, that it is not altered by time. However, for the sake of argument, let us allow the position that theory need not be generic and contingent. Thus, is the content of teacher education based only on locally contingent and constructed 'theories' generated by the teachers themselves? In other words, are there local commonsense theories, grounded in the everyday practices of professionals, rather than derived from university-based research? Here, therefore, is a basis for teacher education which is culturally contingent, and which allows for local cultural configurations based on class, gender, religion, professionalism and ethnicity.

(c) The medium whereby, and/or by whom, this content is transmitted: that is to say, is the content of teacher education:

- based mainly in higher education;
- based mainly in the schools; or
- transmitted mainly at a distance, by print and/or by electronic means, and possibly as commercial packages?

These three dimensions of teacher education – the locus of control, the content, the mode of transmission – will serve as general themes which run through our consideration of teacher education from 1960 to the present. We shall divide this period into three broad phases: (a) Teacher education: certainty; (b) Teacher education: doubt, reflection and reconstruction; and (c) Teacher education: the pedagogical fix and the renewed quest for certainty.

Teacher education: certainty

One of Toulmin's pillars of modernity is certainty. In the age of modernity, the disciplines enabled us to explain the world. Within education, a science of pedagogy emerged, informed particularly by the discipline of psychology. By the 1920s, the dominant theory was that of behaviourism, a theory which resonated well with the metaphor of the telephone, which at that time in the United States was becoming popular: that is, stimulus (the number is dialled), process (the telephone exchange) and response (the telephone rings elsewhere). Edward L. Thorndike is arguably the most well-known behaviourist in education. Born in 1874, he was influenced by William James's *Principles of Psychology*, published in 1890, and he went on to study psychology at Harvard. He began this research by asking children to guess what he was thinking, and he rewarded them if they did so correctly. Sad to say for Thorndike, his experiments with children were disapproved of, and he had to switch to studying chickens. He eventually completed his doctoral dissertation, *Animal Intelligence*, at Columbia University. Thorndike's *Educational Psychology: The Psychology of Learning* was published in 1913. The more confident-sounding *Fundamentals of Learning* was published in 1932. What is important to note about the behaviourists is that, in their explanations, only observable stimuli and responses were allowable. All else was set aside. There was no possible science of the mind. During the same period, developments in statistics enabled the IQ-testing movement to claim that it was possible to measure accurately the academic potential of children. That done, in the interests of meeting their educational needs, it would be possible to create different types of educational provision that would best satisfy those needs. Thus it was that three types of school were created in the United States – one for the hand-minded, one for the general thinker and one for the abstract thinker. But these three types of school were regarded as being socially divisive. In the 1920s, therefore, three tracks were formed to form a single comprehensive high school, thereby ensuring that although children would cease to be segregated from each other socially they would nevertheless be educated according to their needs. Testing made possible this allegedly accurate placement in an appropriate type of school. In sum, more generally, the scientific movement in American education gained pace. Objective precision was said to be possible: in the teaching of the child (informed by behaviourist theory); in the form of the curriculum (aims and objectives); and in assessment (objective testing). But all was not well with this objectivity. As late as 1949, John Dewey, in a letter to Adelbert Ames, wrote:

> I have been convinced for a long time that the obsession of psychologists with quantity is both a cause and effect of the backwardness of that subject. A quantitative statement with no theory to determine what is being measured would justify calling the 'measuring' of all cracks in the plaster of my wall 'science' if it were done with elaborate statistical techniques. To hell with it – but unfortunately they hoodooed the Foundations' Directors, who have little idea of what Scientific Method is, joined with a superstitious respect for what they think is science – with an extra big capital letter.
>
> (Dewey, quoted in Johanningmeier, 1980: 53–4)

All the same, by the 1960s it was claimed that there was a sufficiently robust knowledge-base for the education of teachers. Gage's *Handbook of Research on Teaching*, including his own chapter 'The science of teaching', was published in 1963. Meanwhile, the excesses of behaviourism pointed up by Dewey were giving way to Piaget's genetic epistemology, the culmination of about six decades of research in naturalistic settings. Here too was a general theory, as the term genetic epistemology implies, and as the titles of his books, *The Science of Education* and *The Psychology of the Child*, published in 1970, both suggest. Later, supporters of Vygotsky argued that, rather than cognitive capacities being preprogrammed genetically (the Piagetian view), they emerge and are revealed socioculturally. So culture, cognition and pedagogy are all interdependent (Gordon, 1995). The production of this scientific corpus of knowledge had been a long time coming, and by 1986 teacher educators felt able (in America, at least) to meet their critics.

But first: a detour. When we speak of theory in teacher education, we can usefully differentiate between theory about education and theory for teaching. Take this quotation from McNamara:

> When we visit the dentist we hope that he has a wider view of his [sic] role and is concerned, for instance, about the funding of the Health Service, that he will treat us with consideration and offer an explanation of the treatment we may require, and that he considers all his patients equally without regard to gender or race. All of this expertise, which is an adjunct to professional practice, will count for nothing if he reduces us to agony while drilling a tooth.
>
> (McNamara, 1993: 282)

That said, at issue is the relevance to classroom practice of these about-education matters. They need not necessarily be, as McNamara implies, a mere adjunct to professional practice. But McNamara has alerted us to a very important issue, and it will loom large when, below, we take up the question of the 'reflective practitioner'. For the moment, as we explore some of the modernist reforms in teacher education, it might be helpful to keep in mind whether or not the knowledge-base is:

- to be derived from research which is conducted by academics within the university;
- to be derived from research which is conducted by academics, not necessarily within the university, but also within the schools; and perhaps in collaboration with teachers;
- to be derived from the 'craft' practice of the teachers themselves, a practice which, on reflection, is made explicit in written form and is codified, with or without the assistance of academics.

Let us now set out the broad background to the impetus for reform which began in the early 1980s. In the United States the influential *A Nation at Risk* had suggested that the United States was 'committing an act of unthinking unilateral educational disarmament' (National Commission on Excellence in Education, 1983: 5). As we said earlier, a similar panic-button had been pushed when, in 1957, the Soviet

Sputnik satellite had been launched, thereby prompting a radical reassessment of science education in America. But in the 1980s it was the American economy which was said to be at risk, and this was attributed in no small measure to the failure of its schools; and, by implication, of its faculties and colleges of education. Teacher educators were caught in a double-bind: within the academy they were seen as marginal academics; within the schools they were regarded as distant and irrelevant to the practicalities of teaching. In the United Kingdom similar sentiments were being expressed, and particularly so by the likes of Keith Joseph and former adherents to the *Black Papers* school of thought who all believed that both the moral and the economic decline of Britain could be pinned on woolly-minded progressive teachers, the seeds of whose malpractice had been sown in the colleges of education. Keith Joseph, a Secretary of State for Education in Margaret Thatcher's government, in a speech on teacher training at Durham University in 1982, referred to the 'jargon-ridden theorizing' in teacher education which had served as 'lamentable substitutes for serious thought and training' (Joseph, quoted in Wilkin, 1996: 149). In the United States, meanwhile, no national government initiative was possible. Reform was to come from the universities themselves with the formation of the Holmes Group, to which we now turn.

The Holmes Group comprised a consortium of ninety-six deans of faculties of education which had initial teacher training programmes. Its task was to be two fold: first, academic; and second, political. It first had to convince the public and the rest of the academy that in teacher education there now had accumulated a body of theory and research which could be trusted. In its first report, the Holmes Group asserted that our knowledge of how to teach did not emerge from the common-sense practice of teachers in the schools, but by painstaking and rigorous research in the universities:

> The established professions have, over time, developed a body of specialized knowledge, codified and transmitted through professional education and clinical practice. Their claim to professional status rests on this. For the occupation of teaching, a defensible claim for such special knowledge has emerged only recently. Efforts to reform the preparation of teachers and the profession of teaching must begin, therefore, with the serious work of articulating the knowledge base of the profession and developing the means by which it can be imparted.
>
> (Holmes Group, 1986: 63)

Teacher education should thereafter be based mainly in the universities, and should itself rest on a sound academic foundation, namely the bachelor's degree – in sum, a liberal education which preceded professional education. How to transmit the knowledge-base of teaching was the task of those charged with teaching educational studies and with supervising clinical experience. The teachers in schools were brought in to the university to assist, and even to participate in research. The Group were mindful too that teachers at different stages in their careers – instructors (with no tenure), professional teachers and career professionals (both with tenure) – had different educational needs, and these must be defined and catered for. Here, therefore, teaching ceases to be a 'flat' hierarchy (usually an indication of a profession). A further purpose in *Tomorrow's Teachers* was to generate more appropriate entry procedures, and to revamp in a more comprehensive way how teaching proficiency was to be measured. There were calls, too, for 'minority' applicants to be encouraged to enter teaching, and for support to be afforded them.

This first Holmes Group report is a statement rooted within modernity: the emphasis on abstract and general public theory which is based within the disciplines; the confident assumption that progress is possible; the spatial separation of school and college, of teacher and professor; the assumption that knowing why is as important as knowing how. But it is curious that at the present time, as the structural coherence of the disciplines is under sustained attack, prominent teacher educators should be wishing to reaffirm a generic and research-based epistemology. Those who reassert the natural science research paradigm for teacher education – either because they believe in it and/or because they think it will provide much-needed academic justification for a university-based teacher education – may well be swimming against the cultural tide of postmodernism and its anti-positivist critique (Labaree, 1992: 143–4). By the early 1980s, Toulmin's first pillar of modernity – *certainty* – was looking decidedly unstable. A *clean slate* – his third pillar – was needed in order to shore up the modernist edifice. It was time to reflect and perhaps to construct teacher education anew.

Teacher education: doubt, reflection and reconstruction

By the late 1970s, teacher education seemed set to lose its theoretical basis. That this would happen is not surprising, given the demise of structuralist theories in psychology (behaviourism) and in sociology (functionalism and Marxist theory). In the psychology of education, empiricist process-product research gave way to the narration of teacher cognitions; and sociology of education began to delve into the textualism and post-structuralism which were gaining ground in mainstream sociology and literary theory. There was said to be a 'de-intellectualisation' of teacher education (Wilson, 1989), an anti-disciplinary trend which diluted the theoretical – especially the psychological – basis of pedagogy, weakening its claims as a canon of professional knowledge, reducing it to the status of commonsense practitioner constructs. Stones is worth quoting on this:

> Researchers have also tacitly accepted that teaching is a-theoretical and may be learned on the job. Thus they have looked at how teachers teach now and tried to derive from their studies aspects of teaching that seem to work. These aspects of teaching will then be pronounced examples of good practice. This is a circular process that is essentially conservative. In the lack of a theory of teaching that is independent of the actions of individual teachers, possibilities for progress are very limited.
>
> (Stones, 1992b: 1)

Notwithstanding the concerns of Stones and of Wilson, the grand narratives of the disciplines of psychology, sociology and philosophy began to give way to niche narratives of the reflective practitioner. And for teachers in training, the history of education increasingly came to mean the elaboration of personal histories and biographies; and comparative education moved from the far-away to the here-and-now. In sum, it was claimed that the greater validity and authenticity of the expert teachers' routine everyday knowledge could be represented and made real for the novice. The implicit and tacit knowledge generated by teachers while teaching could be rendered explicit and communicable. But, as we have said, from a political standpoint, if teacher education were to dilute or even to discard its disciplinary basis, then it would be difficult logically to assert that it had the necessary knowledge-base for its claims within academe as a distinct domain.

All this suggests a polarization between two kinds of knowledge: that generated in the academy (abstract, formal, propositional, generalizable, public and written); and that generated by teachers (contingent on time and place; practical; informal and anecdotal, either in oral or written form). Furthermore, teachers' situational knowledge tends to confine itself to matters for teaching rather than matters about education in its broader ethical, social, economic and political contexts. Some argue that there is a need to articulate the two. Examples of this articulation and collaboration are to be found in the Professional Development Schools advocated in the second Holmes Group report, *Tomorrow's Schools*, and in the Oxford Internship Scheme (Benton, 1990). We consider them now, in turn.

Tomorrow's Schools: the second Holmes Group report 1990

In 1990, the Holmes Group, having suggested the formation of Professional Development Schools (PDS) in its first Report, went on to define the principles which should inform it:

- that teaching and learning should be for understanding, an understanding which can be achieved only through active and exploratory learning
- that teaching and learning should occur in a learning community where all collaborate in their learning
- that teachers should be mindful of the wider social inequalities in which their work is set, and that they should act collectively to reduce them, on behalf of their pupils
- that collaborative research into teaching and learning should be undertaken by school and university faculty working as partners, a 'partnership among peers' (Holmes Group, 1990: vii)
- that organizational structures for schools should be devised so as to facilitate these changes.

PDSs share similar goals to professional practice schools (a construct of the American Federation of Teachers) and clinical schools (a construct of the Carnegie report *A Nation Prepared: Teachers for the 21st Century*). The Carnegie report, published in 1986, recommended a medical model: that is, that teacher education be at master's level, over two years, with the second year to be a residency at a clinical school. Here, as in medical training, expert practitioners would work with university-based academics in a common endeavour. (So far, only one country, Finland, provides initial teacher education at the master's-degree level – Simola *et al.*, 1997). But the analogy with medical education can be overplayed. Cuban (1987: 357), drawing on his experience of both teaching hospitals and professional development schools, makes the point that schools have a captive audience – pupils; hospitals do not. The patients choose to enter, and must give their consent to treatment, whether standard or not. And professional development schools would by definition be different from normal schools, and would therefore begin to take on the status of a 'lighthouse' school or a 'laboratory' school. In this sense, they constitute what Hargreaves (1993) refers to as 'safe simulations', destined to succeed as protected enclaves within the turbulence at large in the wider system. But the 1990 version of the PDS was rather different from that put forward in the first Holmes Group report in 1986:

> A Professional Development School must not become a colony settled by the university in the public schools. Rather, it should be an opportunity to join the strengths of the two institutions in pursuit of common purposes, and to combine their intellectual and material resources to more powerfully pursue those purposes.
>
> (Holmes Group, 1990: 51)

In Britain the Department of Education and Science (1992) was to echo this view.

The notion of the PDS has attracted a mixed reception. Whilst it is seen to be well-intentioned, it may nevertheless be viewed less approvingly. Labaree elaborates:

> In *Tomorrow's Teachers*, this institution was portrayed as an extension of the university-based college of education into the schools, through which the university could transmit its scientific knowledge and its prestige to the beleaguered semi-profession of teaching. In *Tomorrow's Schools*, it became an almost mystical scene of collaboration, where the emphasis was put on equality between the partners.
>
> (Labaree, 1995a: 6–7)

In the same vein, Grimmett (1993: 200) wonders: Collaboration: another train? And he asks also if the endorsement of teachers' craft knowledge is but another form of political correctness. How, it can be put, can the university keep a critical distance from the schools? What are these presumed 'common purposes' to which *Tomorrow's Schools* refers? And is it realistic to suppose that, by emulating medical education, teacher education can lay claim to a similar level of professionalism: that is, by referring to trainee teachers as 'interns' undertaking 'residency', by being subjected to 'clinical supervision' while in the 'teaching school', can teacher educators generate in the public a perception that they are on a par with medical educators? All the same, this discursive shift may constitute an important tactic in the strategy to enhance the status of teacher educators with the public (including the schools themselves).

There is another aspect to be considered. It turns on the claim which teacher educators make that they have accumulated a sufficiently robust corpus of knowledge which can convince both the laity and the academy that their monopoly of teacher education is justified. We suggested above that the reflective turn in the epistemological basis of teacher education occurred in the mid-1970s. It is worth revisiting the intellectual roots of this and dwelling for a moment on Alfred Schutz's (1967) concept of 'recipe knowledge'. For Schutz, most of us act habitually, without reflection. We use 'recipe knowledge' which we have acquired over time through socialization. It is only when our taken-for-granted habits come up against new situations – like our first day of school as a child – that we are reminded of the conscious construction of our habitual actions. Then we must try to reflect on the situation. We must make sense of this new objective world and assign to it a subjective meaning, a meaning we may come to share with others, in which case it would become a social construction of reality.

Much of the criticism made by those resisting the anti-disciplinary trend in teacher education is levelled against what is loosely termed as the process of reflection in professional teacher education. There are a number of classifications of reflective practice available. Take Grimmett's (1988: 12–13). First, it can refer to thought about action, which itself can lead to the application of so-called authoritative academic research findings to professional practice. Second, reflection can refer to deliberations and choices about competing definitions of what counts as 'good teaching' in particular classroom contexts. Grimmett's third category includes those types of reflection which draw upon cultural hermeneutics and the social phenomenology of Alfred Schutz (1967), and their refinement by ethnomethodologists (Garfinkel, 1967) and symbolic interactionists.

In order to clarify Grimmett's third category, it is necessary to touch on sociology's recent paradigm wars. Sociological theory until the mid-1960s was dominated by structural functionalism, a 'grand narrative' which purported to explain the modern age. Its eclipse was sudden. Two assertive paradigms vied to fill the theoretical void: social phenomenology (together with ethnomethodology); and Marxist theory. Marxists accused the phenomenologists of confining their gaze to 'definitions of the situation', rather than to the structural causes of the very situation which was being defined. In response, they accused Marxists of that very over-determinism which had been levelled at functionalists. The ethnomethodologists re-emphasised that the 'nature' of reality was slippery, not fixed, and was continuously in process. They served up 'experiments' which purposely 'unsituated' people, shaking up their common sense, de-meaning it, rendering it problematic, causing them to reflect on the situation in order to construct it anew in their minds. And so it is with reflective pedagogy, for it prompts the teacher to render explicit that which is implicit.

Reflective pedagogy has not been without its critics. For example, the difficulty with a reflective pedagogy informed by constructivism, which itself has its roots in social phenomenology and ethnomethodology, is that these 'constructions' of reality – these 'stories' or 'personal narratives' – are all very interesting at the descriptive level, but they amount to little more than making us aware of our commonsense assumptions and constructs about teaching. Their strength is that they have practical relevance, that they are grounded in everyday situations, that they are authentic, and that they render problematic that which hitherto had been merely habitual. But the 'everyday situations' – the teacher, the child, the school, the classroom, the curriculum – are themselves constructions. They are not 'givens' in any natural sense; they only appear so. The theoretical weakness of some forms of reflective pedagogy in teacher education is that these 'givens' remain as given. They are not explained, except in terms of the practitioner's own commonsense theories. In other words, unless the disciplines are brought to bear on these narratives in order to explain them, then teacher education can lapse easily into a self-reflective mode. That is to say, 'Students may be encouraged to "reflect"; but without the controlling procedures of reason that the disciplines deploy, such "reflection" may easily become no more than the airing of personal prejudice or fashionable ideology' (Wilson, 1991: 117). Not that this has gone unrecognized, which introduces a second classification of reflection. Informed by Habermas, a number of teacher educators, whilst retaining the term 'reflection', have called for a more socially critical usage of the term (Carr and Kemmis, 1986), which is to say that we should be mindful of the structural conditions in which the schools and teaching are located, and of the often hidden interests which they serve, even when the language which is used to describe them may appear democratic and progressive.

So far we have said that there are two broad disputes and confusions about the theory and content of teacher education: first, between those who aver the importance of the disciplines in teacher education and those who do not; and second, between those who themselves espouse reflective pedagogy but who enter into conceptual disputes about what reflective pedagogy means. Even so, the evidence that reflective pedagogy has taken hold at the level of practice among teacher educators remains somewhat elusive.

We are now in a position to consider a further approach which attempts to deal with a range of issues which confronted teacher education in the post-*Tomorrow's-Schools* period. These can be summarized thus:

- How can teacher education be both professionally relevant to classroom practice and, at the same time, be intellectually rigorous so that it can stake its claim as being underpinned by a consensual body of knowledge which is both theoretically coherent and empirically based?
- How can teacher education deal with the issue that schools are located in a culture (postmodernism), polity (democracy) and economy (capitalism) which are complex and undergoing constant change?

The example which we now consider is the Oxford Internship Scheme (Benton, 1990; McIntyre and Hagger, 1992; McIntyre, Hagger and Wilkin, 1993; McIntyre, 1995).

The Oxford Internship Scheme

School-based teacher training is by no means new, either in Britain (Gardner, 1993) or in the United States (Cuban, 1987). The monitorial system introduced in England in the nineteenth century was an attempt to produce teachers in the same way that goods were manufactured in a factory. Instead of the factory, the school itself was the site of this production wherein teachers were trained in a highly mechanistic manner in batch-production fashion. Horace Mann, the Secretary to the Board of Education for Massachusetts, reported unfavourably on this monitorial school system after his return from a two-year study of European schools in 1844. He remarked:

I saw many Lancasterian or Monitorial schools in England, Scotland and Ireland; and a few in France. Some mere vestiges of the plan are still to be found in the 'poor schools' of Prussia; but nothing of it remains in Holland, or in many of the German States. It has been abolished in these countries by a universal public opinion . . . one must rise to some comprehension of the vast import and significance of the phrase, 'to educate,' before he [sic] can regard with a sufficiently energetic contempt that boast of Dr. Bell, 'Give me twenty-four pupils of today, and I will give you back twenty-four teachers to-morrow.'

(Mann, 1857: 44)

Cuban, in his commentary on *Tomorrow's Teachers*, suggests that its authors are suffering from 'selective amnesia' about earlier school-based attempts at the reform of teacher education in the United States, citing, for example, the Cardozo Project in Urban Teaching, which trained tens of thousands of teachers, with thousands of university teachers taking part. All this was reported, but no reference to it can be found in *Tomorrow's Teachers*. So, we have been here before.

The Oxford Internship Scheme was a one-year programme for graduates who intended to become secondary school teachers. Each school which participated in the programme would have about ten interns (we should note that they are not merely student teachers), who were there in the school to acquire 'situational knowledge', or 'professional knowledge', which is that knowledge which is embedded in the teacher's (the mentor's) everyday practice, and which may be made explicit for others who are there to acquire it. Put differently, interns would come to acquire the 'craft knowledge' of experienced teachers. About half of the interns' time was in the school and half in the university, but for ten to twelve weeks they remained wholly in the school. The context in which this knowledge-acquisition occurred was deliberately arranged so as to make possible a gradual, non-threatening learning regime for the interns. And there was a structured collaboration among the mentors, the interns and the university-based curriculum tutors. Although the purpose of the school-based training was to enable the interns to acquire professional knowledge, their acquisition of formally coded disciplinary theory was not neglected. The interrelationship between the two was made. Thus there is an appropriate consideration not just of professional knowledge but also of public theory and research. McIntyre and Hagger (1992:

278) refer approvingly to Carr and Kemmis's *Becoming Critical*, and they even see the internship scheme as a way of bringing critical insights to a school in a way which avoids a confrontation with the school itself:

> It would not be reasonable to expect those in positions of power within the bureaucratic hierarchy, such as school principals, to be able to take the lead in helping teachers to examine the system critically, even if as individuals they would value such critical perspectives. Such an initiative can surely be taken more easily by external bodies such as university schools of education, with less immediate vested interests in particular school structures, policies and practices. Schools, however, could well feel threatened by the suggestion of a direct critique to be conducted by such an external body.
>
> (McIntyre and Hagger, 1992: 279)

The university does not itself offer a critique of the system or of individual schools; but, through the interns, it offers teachers the tools for doing so, if they find they need them (p. 280). Thus the interns can seemingly act as messengers of the critical voices within the university.

But not quite. Let us return to theory. The public theories generated within the academy should, in the strict sense, be both consensual and generalizable in their application. Pring (1994: 175), for example, has underlined the difficulties of establishing a theory of pedagogy. Drawing on O'Connor (1957), he has restated the demanding conditions which must be satisfied before the term 'theory' is warranted. Description is not enough. Theory must explain and make predictions, and it must be open to falsification. So far, pedagogical theory has not met these conditions. But this is not seen as overly problematic: if, in the training of teachers, we are concerned with passing on professional, situated or craft knowledge, then all to the good. The difficulty with this reliance solely upon craft knowledge is that it has not been codified, as Hirst (1990) has argued in his commentary upon the Oxford Internship Scheme. In response, McIntyre (1995: 372–3) has stated that very little consensus exists anyway about what shall constitute even the public theories which inform pedagogy in particular, and the institution of education in general; and nor would this be expected, given the inherently political and value-laden 'nature' of education. Therefore, consensus is to some extent contingent upon time and place.

We have made two points. First, the age of disciplinary certainty in teacher education began to be questioned in the mid-1970s. In America, for example, the first reaction by the Holmes Group's *Tomorrow's Teachers* was to reassert the old ways: that is, to separate knowing from doing, theory from practice, and to retain broadly the geographical and hierarchical boundaries between teachers and teacher educators, and the disciplinary boundaries within the 'foundation' subjects of teacher education. Second, in the 1980s, various cultural and intellectual influences were brought to bear on teacher education. The age of postmodernism and consumerism began to disrupt all kinds of boundaries: intellectual boundaries between the disciplines weakened, prompting suggestions that teacher education was becoming de-intellectualized; geographical boundaries between schools and other educational institutions began to blur, and there was talk of partnerships and articulations; in the increasingly marketized public sector, choice and diversity were given official endorsement; and groups which had hitherto been marginalized now raised their concerns for multicultural rights. So the epistemological and spatial geographies of teacher education reflected the broader culture of consumerism, its varieties and niches. And the increasingly pluralistic – not to say individualistic – culture of postmodernism now admits few absolutes. Values are seen as being relative to each other. Thus it is that, more than hitherto, the values held by those entering teacher education will tend to be very diffuse (and this very variety of values will itself obtain among the pupils whom they will go on to teach). Teacher education can no longer assume an homogeneity of value-positions in students. And so it would be appropriate that students should be asked, at the outset, to make explicit their values, and to contrast them with those of their fellow students (Frost, 1993: 138).

Let us revisit the question of reflection. We may ask why the very notion of the 'reflective practitioner' takes root in the minds of professionals during the 1970s and 1980s. Could it be that in the culture of consumption we are required to reflect upon our identities before we go on to choose and to buy those new products and services which will give our lives meaning, if only fleetingly? Is the reflective practitioner simply a part of the individualistic (not to say narcissistic) tendency of the times? That is to say, reflecting is now part of our mind-set. Now: if we come to view all of this postmodernist mélange from a bureaucratic mind-set, or on efficiency criteria, then it might begin to look decidedly messy, with too many blurred categories, with too little certainty, with not enough structure. And if, too, we are concerned to curb expenditure on the welfare state, then even if we were to think that this great variety and mixing of categories is all to the good, it is nevertheless expensive; and perhaps too unaccountable, financially. That being so, it would logically behove us to rethink teacher education, to give it some semblance of structure. And so it was that the government in England and Wales decided to wipe the slate clean, to use Toulmin's metaphor, and, in doing so, to resort to certainty and to systematicity, thereby shoring up Toulmin's three pillars of modernity.

Teacher education: the pedagogical fix and the renewed quest for certainty

The period of reflection, doubt and reconstruction to which we have been referring has by no means settled the matter of what shall comprise teacher education, or of who shall decide upon it; or indeed of who shall deliver it, and where. From an epistemological point of view, we have just referred to the debate between Hirst and McIntyre. But there remains a further complication. The postmodernist critique of knowledge seems to take issue with both Hirst and McIntyre. Of Hirst's position, it would doubt his notion that a consensus within a discipline exists, can exist or even should exist. Of McIntyre's position, which draws upon symbolic interactionism and the social construction of knowledge, it would say that even local narratives and commonsense theories are inadmissible. For what the postmodernists argue is that no representations of reality are possible, whether based on theory which makes universal claims or on 'theory' which is highly contingent on time and place. As for government, set as it is upon curbing expenditure and on controlling the self-serving professions, it faces other choices. Does it deal with the teacher educators by repositioning teacher education in the school, thereby affording more influence to the schoolteachers; and does it begin to despair of the epistemological debates about the knowledge-base of teacher education? In short, does the government try to sort out the intellectual confusion by imposing its own definition of teacher education, thereby reasserting certainty? Clearly, government influences vary. In the United States, for example, the federal government can make few inroads at a national level, but nevertheless informal networks can emerge. In the United Kingdom – at least in England and Wales – it is a quite different matter. Central government has greater powers to impose its will. To illustrate this we turn to the formation of the Teacher Training Agency in England, and to its definition of the national curriculum for initial teacher training.

The Teacher Training Agency

Almost ten years after the National Curriculum in England and Wales was launched, Gillian Shephard, the Secretary of State for Education and Employment in the then Conservative government, stressed the need for momentum and haste in her plans for the reform of initial teacher education. In a press notice (DfEE, 1996a) she stated, 'I make no apology for the speed at which I am taking this forward. The need for improvement is urgent.' This 'momentum', as we have stated, had been set in train by Keith Joseph's reference to the 'jargon-ridden theorizing' in teacher education. Wilkin has analysed persuasively the aftermath of this statement, showing that the public-sector providers thereafter became less focused on the foundation disciplines, giving greater emphasis to school-based competence:

> As early as 1984, in Circular 3/84, the government had made deep inroads into the training institutions at both structural and substantive levels. The strategies and tactics used for this purpose were multiple and comprehensive: compulsory inspection, the loss of power and influence to the schools supported by the shift from theory to practice in the course. And the most powerful incentive of all – the power to close any course which failed to meet the criteria.
>
> (Wilkin, 1996: 52)

Given this sense of urgency, it was not surprising that the government seemed to tire of the consultation process which it had set in train. Its direction was very clear: it was going to free education from theory. Indeed the former Conservative Minister, Cheryl Gillan, speaking of the national curriculum for teachers which was to come, stated: 'The professional framework will not be a dry theoretical construct. It will be firmly rooted in good classroom practice, and will reflect and affect the way teachers routinely think and talk about their work' (DfEE, 1996b: item 56).

Indeed serious doubts have been raised about the TTA's consultation process. Mahony and Hextall have reported on the level of knowledge which respondents had of the 'activities and operations of the TTA' (Mahony and Hextall, 1997a: 2). Their survey included the higher education institutions involved in initial teacher training, the LEAs, and some 170 schools, mainly secondary. Although the TTA seemed to set much store by consultation, there was little heed paid to negotiation: the agenda of the consultative process was set by the TTA; the process whereby responses were weighed and interpreted was unclear; and, 'Even those who were broadly favourable to the policy directions of the Agency expressed concern about the procedures through which these were steered, legitimated and implemented' (Mahony and Hextall, 1997a: 13). For example, the TTA's consultation paper *Revised Requirements for All Courses of Initial Teacher Training* (Teacher Training Agency, 1997), published in February 1997, was barely changed in its final version (DfEE, 1997). Whereas the consultative process which was associated with the introduction of the National Curriculum tended to be somewhat cursory, it nevertheless derived from the policies of an elected government. The TTA remained an unelected body. Members were appointed by ministers, and key stakeholders were said to be without formal representation (Mahony and Hextall, 1997a: 13).

Meanwhile, the UK government had extended the remit of its Office for Standards in Education (OFSTED) so as to allow it to inspect courses of initial teacher training in England and Wales. The OFSTED/TTA (1996: 10) framework contained an elaborate arrangement of areas: these were the central assessed area, namely 'Teaching Competence of Students and of NQTs'; its major contributory area, namely the 'Quality of Training and Assessment of Students'; and other contributory areas, namely the 'Selection and Quality of Student Intake', the 'Quality of Staffing and Learning Resources', and the 'Management and Quality Assurance'. Each type of area had its component cells, some sixteen in all. Each cell had its own set of criteria, giving over 120 criteria in all. Each of the sixteen individual cells was 'normally' to be graded on a four-point scale: 'very good' (1); 'good' (2); 'adequate' (3); and 'poor quality' (4). What should not be overlooked is that here, for the first time, the state, not a professional accreditation body, has laid down the curriculum of a university-based course of professional education.

By 1998, the TTA had made public its final prescription for initial teacher education in its *Circular 4/98 Requirements for Courses of Initial Teacher Training* (DfEE, 1998):

> The curricula specify the essential core of knowledge, understanding and skills which trainees must be taught and be able to use in relation to English, mathematics, science and information and communications technology. They do not cover everything that a trainee teacher will be taught, nor do they repeat the content of the pupils' National Curriculum. Rather, they set out the core

of what trainees need to be taught, know and be able to do if they are to teach the pupils' curriculum effectively. *The curricula do not specify a course model or scheme of work and it is for providers to decide how training is best delivered.* Providers should use the curricula as the basis for designing courses which are coherent, intellectually stimulating and professionally challenging. (italics added)

We can note here the Agency's reference to the discretion of the teacher educators whilst at the same time framing them within its own requirements, as the italicized section of the quotation suggests. But the message is clear: by the government's own admission, there is to be great specificity: 'The standards set out in this document replace the more general "competences" set out in DFE *Circular 9/92* and *14/93* and DFE *Teacher Training Circular Letter 1/96*' (DfEE, 1998: annexe A). It goes on:

The standards have been written to be specific, explicit and assessable, and are designed to provide a clear basis for the reliable and consistent award of Qualified Teacher Status, regardless of the training route or type of training leading to QTS. To achieve this purpose, each standard has been set out discretely.

(Annexe A: para. D)

But, again, there is a rhetorical appeal to professional discretion:

Professionalism, however, implies more than meeting a series of discrete standards. It is necessary to consider the standards as a whole to appreciate the creativity, commitment, energy and enthusiasm which teaching demands, and the intellectual and managerial skills required of the effective professional.

(ibid.)

If, therefore, we recall Toulmin's two pillars of modernity – certainty and specificity – then the TTA's new standards surely represent an attempt to reaffirm both. But it may all turn out to be illusory, a 'dead certainty' (Hargeaves, 1993), a last-ditch attempt to render certain and specific a matter which is too complex to be reduced to simple specifics:

We do live in a diversified and polymorphic world where every attempt to insert consensus proves to be but a continuation of discord by other means. *This world has undergone for a long time . . . a process of thorough and relentless 'uncertainization'.*

(Bauman, 1997: 203: italics added)

In Chapter 2, we argued that organizations within the same 'field' approximate to the same structure. The New Public Management (Ferlie *et al.*, 1996) represents for some a new structural form in the governance of the welfare state. Within the field of education, at the level of policy, it is possible to see isomorphic forms which combine both central control over strategy and local devolution of the tactics to achieve them. The central control over curriculum and assessment introduced by the National Curriculum in England was required in order for a regulated market to work. The government's intention was never to provide a choice of product, only of providers: that is to say, of schools. The problem of how to get the measure of schools was solved at a stroke by national testing and the league tables to which it would give rise. Now a market for initial teacher training is very likely. Whilst the initial move towards a more competence-based and school-based training – such as the Oxford Internship Scheme – was made for sound pedagogical reasons, it appears to have been co-opted by the former Conservative government for political reasons. Frost's timely warning has been largely borne out:

It would be a tragedy indeed if all the effort and ingenuity aimed at developing the reflective practitioner approach to professional development merely served to legitimize the imposition of a narrow, behaviourist systems approach.

(Frost 1993: 135)

Teacher educators have so far set much store by the valid assessments of students. This has had the effect of minimizing the reliability of assessment grades, thereby making it difficult for students (and providers) to be compared objectively. Given that the former Conservative government's thinking on education had been framed within a market metaphor, the lack of comparable and objective indicators of institutional performance was not allowing a government-controlled market of providers to emerge. That is, would-be applicants for training programmes lacked reliable information on the 'product'. The new National Curriculum and assessment for initial teacher training was to remove this obstacle. Moreover there was then a clear articulation possible between the inspection of the national initial teacher training curriculum (by OFSTED) and the audit-cum-funding allocations (by the TTA). Although the reliability of these assessments may still prove to be overly weak, the government can portray them as reliable measures of institutional training in order to allocate students and funds.

Here, too, we begin to see clear evidence of Toulmin's second pillar of modernity, namely formal rationality or systematicity. First, the teaching profession is to be differentiated (and here there are parallels with the Holmes Group): 'new teacher, expect [sic] classroom teacher, subject leader and headteacher' (DfEE, 1996b: item 55). In sum, the national standards for the teachers in training in the 1990s are the counterpart to the national core curriculum for the pupils in the 1980s. In the wake of what was regarded by government as a post-modern 'mess' of progressivism, relativism and constructivism, now a modernist neo-behaviourism lights the way ahead, with signposts to the past. The way forward is now to be back to basics, for pupils and teacher educators alike. It is a clear case of remodernization. It seems that government believes that the fractured culture of postmodernism can be contained, and that the theoretical disputes within the academy can be set aside. Graham (1998: 13) argues that what emerged during the early 1990s in England and Wales was not so much a post-Fordist approach to the managerment of teachers as a neo-Fordist approach: cost-cutting; reducing the social wage; curbing the power of unions; and the imposition of low-skill, low-wage production. This, argues Graham, is not the post-Fordist solution which the economy needs. That is to say, the economy needs a 'functionally flexible, highly skilled and well paid workforce, working consensually with democratised management processes' (Graham, 1998: 13). All that said, however, the push in England and Wales for greater technical rationality appears not to have had the intended consequence among teacher educators. Whitty (1999: 7–8) refers to the findings of the Modes of Teacher Education (MOTE) study which reported that in 1995–96 some 46 per cent of teacher education courses still adhered to the idea of the reflective practitioner, a percentage down from 57 per cent in 1990–91. Only 11 per cent in 1995–96 supported the 'competency' model.

But this is England. In Australia another attempt to define national standards is under way, for the first time. The Australian Council of Deans of Education's *Preparing a Profession* (Report of the National Standards and Guidelines for Initial Teacher Education Project) was published in 1998. The guidelines purport:

to identify a comprehensive array of qualities expected of new graduates of initial teacher education programs. These qualities are held to be fundamental for any beginning teacher in this country ... It has been essential to recommend a framework that makes possible substantive attention to the critical components of initial teacher education. Within that framework, there is substantial hope for variation, allowing for both undergraduate and graduate entry course designs. In general the National Standards and Guidelines for Initial Teacher Education focus on areas to be covered in course designs without prescribing how this should be done. We believe that this is an essential provision if diversity is to be both sustained and promoted.

(pp. 1–2)

All this is notwithstanding the very diversity of state and Commonwealth interests in Australia. The report lists over fifty graduate standards covering the following: general professional standards; duty of care, health and safety; students and their communities; indigenous education; content studies; curriculum; literacy; numeracy: teaching and learning; relationships with learners and behaviour management; technology; assessment; working with others; working with the schools and system. It proposes three options for an accreditation procedure (p. 48), none of which, unlike in England, is defined and controlled by government.

Both the TTA's prescriptions and the Australian Council of Deans of Education's recommendations seek to define national standards with precision. This can be contrasted with the Danish Ministry of Education's (1999) *The Education of Teachers for the Danish 'Folkskole' at Colleges of Education*. In many respects it accords with that Golden Age of certainty and of confidence which we discussed earlier in the section *Teacher Education: Certainty*. Consider, first, its orientation to the colleges of education: 'The ministry has laid down broad guidelines for the overall objectives and aims of the individual subjects, within which the individual institutions are allowed great autonomy as to the duration and scope of the individual courses' (Danish Ministry of Education, 1999: 1). The syllabus for the four-year courses comprises:

1. Religious studies and philosophy;
2. Four specialised subjects taught in the Folkskolen, with a thesis related to one in the last semester;

3. The educational subject areas: educational theory (pedagogy), educational philosophy (general didactics), psychology and educational sociology (school and society) ; and
4. Teaching practice.

(p. 2)

It goes on to state one of the 'characteristic features' of the course,

> It should be noted that to a very large extent teachers in the Folkskole are free to plan and carry out their teaching within the general framework laid down by the ministry and that the aim of teacher education therefore is to educate teachers to exercise this freedom of approach.

(p. 3)

The references to 'educational theory (pedagogy), educational philosophy (general didactics), psychology and educational sociology (school and society)' hark back to a time long lost in England and Wales; and, as for the matter of trusting the colleges of education to do their work free from the close scrutiny of the government, their English counterparts would surely be green with envy.

In the United States, meanwhile, yet a further attempt to systematize teacher education was being aired in the third Holmes Group (1995) report, *Tomorrow's Schools of Education*. It centres upon the importance of the professional development schools which the previous two reports had set much store by. Of the PDS, the report states:

> The PDS is not, we repeat, IS NOT, just another project for the education school. It must be woven into the very fabric of the TSE [*Tomorrow's Schools of Education*], its many strands combining with those of the institution's other programs . . . The education school may, in fact, have to trim the breadth of other outside involvements and researchers may have to submit to some restraints so that they focus more on their investigations through the PDS prism.
>
> (Holmes Group, 1995: 86, with original capitalization)

The tone of the report is somewhat populist and self-critical of schools of education. There is little reference to specific academic research and commentary. It sees the role of the university school of education as being one of teacher education, and more particularly concerned with teacher education at the level of schools, rather than beyond. It calls, therefore, for a narrowing of the remit of schools of education, and makes much of the interdependence, team-work and commonality of purpose of schools and universities in the training of teachers. In this endeavour – and here it is of a piece with the TTA's and the Australian recommendations – it calls for a 'core curriculum' (entitled *The Core of Learning: What All Educators Must Know* (p. 70)) for educators at initial and advanced levels: 'Our priority will be on program quality for those working to improve learning' (p. 15). The hiring policies of schools of education, therefore, would do well to reflect this declared new agenda. And, in a further attempt at the consolidation of national standards, American teacher education saw in 1996 the formation of the Holmes Partnership. The original Holmes Group joined with the following organizations: the American Association of Colleges of Teacher Education, the National Education Association, the American Federation of Teachers, the American Association of School Administrators, the National Policy Board for Educational Administration, the National Staff Development Council, and – importantly – the National Board for Professional Teaching Standards (NBPTS). The NBPTS is an independent body which was formed in 1987 in the aftermath of the Carnegie Corporation's Task Force report *A Nation Prepared: Teachers for the 21st Century*. Like its legal and medical counterparts, it purports to define what teachers shall know, and it serves also as a regulatory body, with powers of accreditation. Its seminal publication is *What Teachers Should Know and Be Able to Do*.

Tomorrow's Schools of Education has attracted strong criticism, most notably from Labaree (1995b; 1999). He regards it as muddled, contradictory, populist and intellectually thin. The report is seen as being overly concerned with narrow notions of competence – an 'industrial-style research and development' approach:

> The classic attributes of a university – theory-driven research, graduate education, academic autonomy – are now seen as detrimental to the mission laid out for the ideal education school, which is expected to be centred relentlessly on applied knowledge, teacher preparation, and problems of practice.
>
> (Labaree, 1995b: 170)

This, for Labaree, is not to deny the importance of pedagogical training, but is a plea for some distancing theoretically from everyday practice in

Table 3 Modernist reforms of teacher education: a summary

	Teacher education: certainty	Teacher education: reflection and reconstruction	Teacher education: renewed quest for certainty
Locus of control:	Higher education	Higher education & professional bodies	Government or profession & higher education
Curriculum	*Theory:* disciplinary knowledge in psychology, sociology, history and philosophy *Methodology:* empirical & quantitative	*Theory:* teacher narratives; constructivist theory; reflective practitioner *Methodology:* ethnography, action research and case study	*Theory:* not made explicit, but implicit in competences; best practice; evidence-based
Mode of transmission:	Faculties and colleges	Professional development schools; mentoring partnerships; school–higher education partnerships	Professional development schools; mentoring partnerships; school–higher education partnerships
Influences:	Fordism; modernist culture; the disciplines	Consumerism and the 'self'; differences and equity; reactions against positivism	Economic globalization; new managerialism; formal rationality
Policy exemplars	*Tomorrow's Teachers* (USA, 1986)	*Tomorrow's Schools* (USA, 1990) ; The Oxford Internship Scheme	Government TTA (England and Wales, 1998)	*Higher education: Preparing a Profession* (Australia, 1998); National Board for Professional Teaching Standards (USA)

schools. On research, Labaree takes issue with the report's call to locate research only within the problems of practice. He suggests also that we should proceed to 'think big about the roots and nature of educational problems and to pursue a wide range of scholarly enquiries in order to develop theories for understanding these problems' (p. 199). Here he is of like mind to those who espouse a view of reflective practice which admits a socially critical analysis of teacher education rather than a focus only upon the pedagogical means of teaching practice itself.

Summary

These are uncertain times. Education is necessarily part of them. Within teacher education, different interest groups have different agendas. First, some governments seek to curb expenditure on education whilst retaining control over it, and this includes teacher education. But, in this quest for efficiency, government must confront, accommodate or convince teacher educators that its interventions are both necessary and appropriate. So teacher educators seek to guard against what they see as heavy-handed interventions by the state – especially, in England, by the Teacher Training Agency. In other countries – notably the United States and Australia – professional bodies have attempted to construct their own national standards. And elsewhere, as in Denmark, the Danish Ministry of Education exerts by comparison a very light touch. But for the most part the attempts to systematize teacher education have been mixed, not to say confusing, as with the Holmes Group's various reports. In other words, the pillars of modernity – certainty, systematicity and the clean slate – have been shored up, whether by government or by teacher educators. Something, therefore, is being seen to be done. Table 3 summarizes the various types of reform to which we have referred.

Notwithstanding the various attempts to systematize teacher education, Bauman and others have argued that certainty is a rather difficult matter to nail down these days, for a number of reasons. Postmodernist culture admits few certainties, and so teacher education faces the task of coming up with 'generic' theory, practice, values, skills and competences – whatever – in a world wherein agreement is both difficult and short-lived. On the one hand, teacher educators are caught between governments which seek cheap certainties; and, on the other, the wider academy, which may have doubts that teacher educators can cut it academically. And in all this there is a sense of urgency: governments need to be seen to be doing something – anything – about the effects of deeply rooted structural changes which are at once economic, cultural and intellectual.

The English way has been the quick fix, imposed from the centre. Whether or not this portends an international trend is a moot point: Moon (1998: 29) regards the approach in England – 'its combination of regulation and inspection' – as 'unique'. But the very term in England which is used to describe the teacher educator – the 'provider', not the 'university'; not even the 'school' – suggests that, if government-defined national criteria can be met, then it is open to any 'provider' – real or virtual, public or private, national or international – to come up with the goods, so to say. Here, therefore, beckons the market, which is now insinuating itself within education. And the market will surely throw up different forms of schooling. Already there are speculations that within the next twenty-five years we shall witness new market-driven differentiated structures for the formal education of children: from the private school, to the specialized school, to the home-school, and – for many in the urban areas – the custodial school (Hargreaves, 1997). And governments, in their quest to cut expenditure, may well support this reinstitutionalization of formal education Any such restructuring of formal education would have great consequences for the education of teachers, for it too, logically, might itself become much more diversified than is now the case. Atop this diversified market would sit an agency of accreditation and regulation, trusted by the public, endorsed by the academy. Who would control any such agency is the central question. In England, the government has already staked its claim; elsewhere, as in Australia and in the United States, the teacher educators have begun to coalesce within national agencies, and they have begun to codify what teachers shall know, thereby hoping to keep governments at bay, trying to render simple what is complex, seeking certainty amidst confusion.

Chapter 5

Psychology

An agent of modernity in teacher education?

In this chapter we explore how psychology has positioned itself as an agent of modernity, offering cures for uncertainty and providing a rationale for governments' modernising projects in education. We consider how psychology might be most usefully critiqued; and how a more hermeneutic version of psychology might support teachers as they interpret and respond to the demands of practice. These analyses are rooted in a concern with supporting teachers as they construct and use the intellectual and social resources available to them. To that end it is argued that multidisciplinary work may be usefully carried out in partnerships between education professionals in order to strengthen the field, professionals within it and teacher education.

Teaching as pedagogy

Let's try this contestable definition of teaching. Teaching, in government-funded schools, aims at developing the dispositions of pupils so that they become willing learners of the curricula selected for them. Consequently teaching differs from mere curriculum delivery because the development of dispositions to engage with curricula marks the interactive nature of teaching. Interactive teaching requires teachers to focus on *how* pupils tackle learning opportunities and construct understandings, and on *how* they might be supported as learners. Successful teaching, according to this definition, produces pupils with dispositions to approach novel but cognate learning opportunities, whether in school or outside it, with confident curiosity and the wherewithal to begin to deal with them (Anning and Edwards, 1999; Boaler, 1997; De Corte *et al.*, 1996).

Teaching, in this definition, includes both knowledge of curriculum and knowledge of how learners can be helped to connect and engage with it. It is a definition of teaching which includes both didactics and pedagogy in their mainland European sense as respectively analysis of the curriculum subject and analysis of learners and learning opportunities (Leach and Moon, 1999; Tochon and Munby, 1993). Because of attention to how learners engage with the act of teaching, it also allows consideration of curricular values and the development among learners of a capacity to analyse and critique what passes for acceptable knowledge in curricula. Here the definition of teaching approaches the concerns of critical pedagogy found most extensively in the North American and Australian education literature (Giroux, 1989; Smyth, 1991, 1995, 1998), but it does not necessarily make them central to it. It is perhaps here that the version of pedagogy being described is most contestable.

Interestingly, 'pedagogy' is a little-used term in UK education (Simon, 1999). None the less British understandings of pedagogy, when the term is used there, seem closer to those mainland European definitions which emphasize the interactivity of teaching and learning (Tochon, 2000; Edwards, 2001) and the engagement of the learner in the joint activity of teaching and learning. Pedagogy in these definitions, and in a context dominated by agreed curricula, seems to stand for a form of teaching which continuously attends to the sense-making of the learners in order to make possible their participation in the language-games represented by curricula and enhance their sense of self-efficacy as learners. Pedagogically oriented teaching in this definition is therefore a complex and risky activity.

Its complexity lies largely in the extent to which teaching depends on skilful interpretations of learners and the contexts of learning and careful negotiations of possible meanings with those learners. Its riskiness is evident in the responsibilities that teachers carry for learners' induction into the current language-games embedded in curricula and the public nature of the negotiations of meaning undertaken as teaching (Doyle, 1986; Bruner, 1996a).Teaching as pedagogy in the UK sense outlined here demands that participants engage with each other in a process of sense-making which has implications for the identity of both teachers and pupils. For example, teachers intend that learners will be able to interpret the demands of a classroom activity in increasingly informed ways and will demonstrate the capacity to respond appropriately – e.g. pupils are able to see and respond in fresh ways. Teachers too are likely to enhance their stocks of practical knowledge with the passing of each teaching event, and perhaps, like pupils, are able to see and respond in newly informed ways. But teachers' identity shifts and any resulting vulnerability are not the focus of the pedagogical interaction and are usually rendered invisible.

Teaching, in this social constructivist model, is a complex personal interaction requiring teachers to take a degree of risk, to destabilize learners' understandings and to assist them as they construct more appropriate responses. However, pedagogic relationships between teachers and pupils in England and Wales are embedded in policy contexts of public accountability and performed in public arenas which heighten teachers' vulnerability and which are arguably better suited to curriculum delivery and rote learning than risky interactive teaching.

Teaching as curriculum engagement and the development of pupils' dispositions to tackle novelty can be seen, in summary, as the induction of learners into the selected practices of a culture as filtered by schools as institutions. Consequently individual teachers are positioned as personally vulnerable but expert agents with responsibilities for the mediation of specific forms of culture. If this definition holds, individual teachers' pedagogical acts in classrooms are central to the UK government's modernizing agenda which depends heavily on the notions of education as the key to social inclusion and of social inclusion as engagement in economic activity. A great deal therefore rests on the pedagogy of publicly vulnerable individual teachers, with the result that their pedagogy needs to be regulated. There is clear evidence in England of the mechanisms for shaping the minds and actions of teachers. They are found, for example, in initial teacher training where the emphasis is on assessment of teaching performance, strict adherence to long- and short-term planning and avoidance of the risks of a pedagogy that might involve responding spontaneously and interactively to pupils while teaching (Edwards, 1998; Edwards and Ogden, 1998a).

It is unsurprising, therefore, that English government agencies are seeking clear definitions of pedagogy. Interest was flagged first in a lecture in 1996 by the then head of the TTA (Millett, 1996) which attacked teachers' 'personally arrived at pedagogies'. Subsequent pronouncements pointed to the need to attend to the science of teaching and the certainties it might offer (for example Reynolds, 1998). It seemed that a return to the social science bases of initial teacher education, with a particular focus on particular forms of the psychological bases of pedagogy was likely. It would not be the first time, as we shall see later, that a branch of psychology had been called upon to produce a socially homogenizing solution to the social and economic challenges of modernity. The success of some of the versions invoked so far in education has, however, been questionable. None the less the UK's social homogeneity, or rather social inclusion, agenda is pressing and it is understandable that some of those with a responsibility for the pace of change are turning to a science which remains eager to prove its utility to policy-makers.

Pedagogy for what?

The idea that compulsory schooling is an important mechanism for social inclusion and ultimately social control is not new (Walkerdine, 1984). However, representations of the social inclusion agenda in relation to compulsory and post-compulsory education vary across cultures and necessarily capture current and local preoccupations. Representations range from the goals of 'independence, knowledge of right and wrong, respect for property, honesty, and respect for those in authority' voiced by Lortie's teachers (Lortie, 1975: 112) to South Africa's recent agenda for stakeholder participation and local capacity building (South African Government Publication, 1996 cited in Moon, 1998), and include the present Norwegian curriculum framework which focuses on developing the creative, co-operating and environmentally responsible individual (Dalin and Rust, 1996). The current UK agenda for social inclusion is, by contrast with South Africa and Norway, quite narrow: addressing the problems of late capitalism by connecting curriculum delivery with employment opportunities and participation in the economic life of the state.

Giddens's gloss on late twentieth-century social democratic politics argues, however, that in addition to a focus on work, agendas for social inclusion must include provision for those who can't work and recognize 'the wider diversity of goals life has to offer' (Giddens, 1998: 110). It is, none the less, currently difficult to recognize any evidence of these goals in the school lives of even the youngest pupils in England and Wales. Instead the emphasis is on the delivery of core numeracy and literacy curricula, and classroom homogeneity is the unspoken assumption lying behind the pedagogies required of elementary school teachers. For example, the 1997 guidelines for initial teacher training made no reference to English as an Additional Language (Teacher Training Agency, 1997). Equally there is little evidence to suggest that the relationship between the knowledge delivered through curricula in schools can seamlessly enhance the capacity of a flexible workforce.

Initial teacher education in England and Wales has been an important lever in various attempts by governments to control classroom practices over the last two decades (Wilkin, 1996). However, under the remit given to the TTA since 1991 the control of the lever itself has become extraordinarily tight (Jacques, 1998). In summary, teacher educators have been derided while their work has been placed under ever more stringent control by government agencies (Gilroy, 1992; Richards, 1998). Furthermore, increasingly in line with the particular version of social inclusion prevailing in England and Wales, teacher educators are required to focus less on a form of pedagogy which emphasizes how student teachers might support the development of young learners, and more on their capacity to deliver the prescribed curriculum (Richards, Harling and Webb, 1997).

Recent UK governments appear therefore to have combined the rhetorics of social inclusion, economic participation and global competitiveness and seem to have placed responsibility for success in these fields on effective curriculum delivery and hence with educationists whether engaged in classroom teaching, teacher education or educational research. But the responsibility of education professionals is not backed by strong professional agency. In Bourdieu's terms (Bourdieu, 1977) the *field* (of educational practice) is not easily open to contention, while the *habitus* (or dispositions and wherewithal to respond) of practitioners, whether in schools or universities, is limited. Educational practitioners may have responsibility, but it is a responsibility in which individual agency (i.e. responsible action), whether for risky interactive pedagogy or for any other deviation from the government line on pedagogy, is severely curtailed.

The pedagogy currently being validated by national inspection processes in English schools and teacher training programmes is, in the case of elementary school numeracy and literacy, provided as part of curricular requirements. At the same time government advisers revive old debates as new proclamations tell us that teaching is a science and not an art (Reynolds, 1998). It is but a short step from such statements to a turn to psychology as the educational fixer and director of the actions of agents, i.e. teachers. Psychology is well placed to be taken up as the problem-solving science of social inclusion. Indeed the discipline is arguably, in part at least, premised on such a function. But can psychology as the 'appliance of science' in classrooms actually provide solutions to those problems of late modernity that have been landed at the feet of educationists?

Psychology: the neurotic discipline?

Psychoanalytic theory describes neurosis as 'an outward manifestation of deep-seated intrapsychic conflicts that were set up in early life' (McGuffin, 1987: 472). The conflicts and weaknesses that lie behind the emergence of experimental psychology as the dominant strand in the current version of the discipline have been well documented (Harré, 1998; Harris, 1997; Koch, 1959). Sites of early intrapsychic conflict in the discipline included, for example, the marginalization of complex and potentially messy Freudian psychoanalytic theory in North America by the US mental hygienists just after the First World War (see, for example, how the relative contributions of Freud and the mental hygienists to educational psychology are treated in a popular US text for teachers, Blair, Jones and Simpson, 1954) and the appropriation of the work of Binet and Simon on the educational capabilities of children to the assessment of 'intelligence' for selection for tracking and the selecting out of racially and intellectually inferior pupils in Californian schools in the 1930s (Chapman, 1981). Meanwhile in England the caution of some psychologists over the predictive power of intelligence tests in the 1940s (Thom, 1984) was overridden by a political agenda which had begun to see children's intelligence as a national resource which was being constrained by a class-based selective school system. In this argument, intelligence tests could ensure equality of opportunity in a reformed system of schooling.

Psychology, essentially a healing discipline, albeit within an Enlightenment tradition, appears to have found itself positioned in its search for acceptance and the funding it brings as a cure for the fragmentation and uncertainty of aspects of modernity. Its consequent route towards the modernist grail of certainty, prediction and control (Gergen, 1992; Polkinghorne, 1992) led it initially to the psychometric measurement of innate capacities and to behaviourism as a means of controlling the shifts and uncertainties of the displaced, or at least deroutinized, populations of North America and ultimately wartime Europe. Surprisingly, however, for a discipline which purports to concern itself with the individual, experimental psychology drains the subjective from the subject to objectify him or her as a feature to be manipulated.

Its rapid positioning as the scientific cure for social fragmentation and uncertainty as the problems of modernity led psychology, as represented in the laboratories of American universities, to seek premature scientific respectability. Koch, for example, argued that 'psychology was unique in the extent to which its institutionalization preceded its content and its methods preceded its problems' (Koch, 1959: 783). In its neurotic search for respectability, psychology in the 1920s and 1930s turned to the mathematical precision of the machines that were then routinizing working life and allowing the calculations of cause and effect so necessary to a science of prediction and control. Having found its (already outmoded) method, psychology set about the accumulation of segments of knowledge in an attempt to construct a knowledge-base of universal objective truth, which, even by the most partisan observer convinced of the universality of, for example, inter-personal phenomena, can only be seen to be partial. Importantly, its emphasis on the rapid accumulation of knowledge has meant that psychology has not encouraged disciplinary self-criticism. In Lakatos's terms (see Chapter 3 above) the protective belt of assumptions and hypotheses around the core of psychology's research programme has focused more on the protection of a vulnerable core than on being the site in which the language-games of psychology are critically interrogated.

This somewhat cursory analysis is not to argue that psychology is a malign discipline; rather one that has itself been socially constructed. Its construction has tied it to that aspect of modernity which has sought the soothing balm of essential certitude. But there is no sign of the grail being found; as Giddens argues, 'the equation of knowledge with certitude has turned out to be misconceived' (Giddens, 1990: 39). How might psychology come to recognize this misconception and learn to deal with uncertainty? The treatment for neurosis starts with the eventual conscious awareness of intrapsychic conflict (McGuffin, 1987). This route may not be an easy one for psychology as modernist science: Bauman reminds us that 'Modernity had the uncanny capacity for thwarting self-examination' (Bauman, 1993: 3).

Instead, in line with a homogenizing agenda which is to be achieved at a rapid pace, it is to the non-reflective psychology of certainty, prediction and control that UK proponents of teaching as a science currently turn. In doing so they appear oblivious to the reasons given to explain why psychology, along with the other foundation disciplines of sociology, philosophy and history, was eradicated from teacher train-ing programmes in England and Wales in the 1980s through a series of government guidelines which started in 1984 (DES, 1984). The argu-ment of the 1980s rested largely on the apparent irrelevance of these disciplines to the craft of teaching. The decision that psychology is irrelevant to the study of how children may be helped to learn does at first glance appear absurd. Perhaps, therefore, the relationship between psychology and educational practice is worth examining.

Psychology in education

Educational policy-makers appear to be fickle friends for psychology. They invoke the discipline when a scientific basis to policy is required and ignore it when convenient. In contrast the relationship between psychology and the practice of teaching is more clear cut. It is a distant one.

Psychology as an applied science can offer some broad heuristics which have the potential to inform teachers' practical decision-making. These include, for example, understandings of motivation such as attribution theory (Weiner, 1986); the social psychology of groups (Sharan, 1980; Slavin, 1983); memory (Baddeley, 1990; Tulving, 1983); and social (or anti-social) behaviour (Schaffer, 1996). But evidence from those elements of the science most associated with the study of human learning rarely does inform the professional practices of teachers. The difficulty perhaps lies in the need for new toolkits, or solutions, to work with rather than against existing cultures and perhaps assist the adjustment of these cultures to new initiatives (Cole, 1995). When we think about changing teaching in this way we are reminded of the heterogeneity of rooms full of pupils and of the cohorts of teachers who are interacting with them. Psychology failed to serve education well because the version offered in the 1960s and 1970s was all too often disembedded and distanced from local problems. Its success with policy-makers depended on the universal principles it offered rather than the evidence that might inform local toolkits. There were, of course, notable exceptions found in good educationally grounded forms of psychology (e.g. Stones, 1992a) but these too were swept away, unlamented by most practitioners, while teacher training was made ready for a focus on what should be taught to pupils in schools.

Psychology the problem-solver and seeker of certainty did not, however, disappear from the policy arena and was called upon to help shape educational provision in England and Wales during the 1980s and 1990s. Assessment, though mainly criterion-referenced testing of curriculum knowledge, because of its relation to standards and public accountability became an important teacher skill. More recently psychologists' research into the teaching of reading has provided a post-hoc validation of the British government's National Literacy

Strategy in England (Beard, 1999, 2000). Meanwhile psychology, having rubbed shoulders with systems theory, maintained much of its influence in the field of special educational needs and school inclusion (Miller and Leyden, 1999).

However, a telling case study of how psychology has been taken up by policy-makers and translated to suit the ends of policy is the changing meaning of 'match' (Desforges, 1985) since the early 1980s. It is here that we observe the relationship between psychology and policy and see played out Kvale's observation that 'power is knowledge' i.e. those in power can select and shape the knowledge available (Kvale, 1992: 39).

'Match' first entered the educational vocabulary in the wake of the Plowden report on primary education (CACE, 1967). The report referred to Piaget's work on how knowledge develops in children's minds, in order to give scientific weight to the practical proposals it was making. Subsequent interpretations of Piaget's writings, given prominence by the report, encouraged teachers to consider the match between what they might expect an individual child to be able to do and the child's actual developmental *readiness* for the activity. Driven by fairly naive interpretations of the Piagetian concepts of assimilation, accommodation and equilibration (which had not been offered as a basis for pedagogy by Piaget), this version of match led teachers to attempt to ensure that each activity they planned contained a novel element which would trigger disequilibration and hence accommodation. Match, loosely defined as capturing the learning opportunity, therefore lay at the core of child-centred education and provided a rationale for believing that a class consisted of thirty or more individuals constructing their personal understandings of the continuously novel experiences made available to them.

In child-centred practice, constructivism and relativism appeared to be in tandem and hence open to the attacks of the Black Papers (Cox and Dyson, 1971). But Piaget was not a relativist. His lifework aimed at producing an understanding of how specific forms of knowledge develop in human minds which was itself universal. In a similar vein Walkerdine's analysis of Piaget's influence on early education (Walkerdine, 1984) recalls the normalizing uses of developmental psychology and the impact of Piaget's work on teachers' expectations of children at different stages of development. In practice very few teachers operated as if working individually to each child's pace, but as Walkerdine noted they used Piagetian vocabulary to explain their expectations for their classes, a practice also used by mentors when talking with student teachers (Edwards and Collison, 1995). In the Plowden report psychology had, once more, been summoned to the defence of policy and misappropriated in much the same way as Binet's work on individuals had been used to underpin policies of educational tracking in the USA in the 1930s.

The insertion of match into the vocabulary of curriculum delivery during the 1980s even more clearly demonstrates Kvale's inversion of the more commonly recognized relationship between power and knowledge in how psychology has been used. A thoughtful study of just how difficult teachers found constructivist teaching by Bennett *et al.* (1984) moved understandings of match from its Piagetian concerns with the learner to a focus on effective engagement of children with curricula through careful task design. Their analysis of (1) the processes of children's learning drawing heavily on the work of the cognitive psychologist Norman (Norman, 1978) and (2) classroom tasks by way of Doyle (see Doyle 1986 for an overview) did not attempt to simplify the role of teachers, but it did demystify it while maintaining a framing which was both cognitivist and social constructivist.

The problems with curriculum coverage that the study revealed, albeit from a small sample of schools, raised concerns about ineffective curriculum delivery which resonated with preparations for the introduction of the National Curriculum into English and Welsh schools in 1989. Matching, by the late 1980s, became translated into the effective delivery of the normalizing curriculum. This translation did not draw upon the measured analyses carried out by Bennett and his colleagues in their 1984 study. There they had emphasized the need for attention to how children constructed understandings of the curriculum, and criticized teaching which focused on delivery at the expense of learning. Instead match, taken up in policy terms, was decontextualized so that teaching became, by the late 1990s, the delivery of commodified segments of knowledge within predetermined timescales which emphasized pace and curriculum coverage.

Psychology, lacking the capacity for sociopolitical analyses, operating as the science which allows governments to invoke it when useful to justify policies and the allocation of educational opportunities, and positioned at a distance from teachers, actually has little direct impact on the practice of teaching. As a discipline it appears in an impasse in relation to education. Its problem-solving mission is not intrinsic to the practices of teachers. Is there then a way forward in which psychology might usefully connect with the practices of teaching and inform teacher education?

It would seem that a first step might be towards self-conscious aware-ness of how it is positioned as a discipline in relation to both policy and practice. Currently two routes appear to be open to psychologists seeking critical analyses of psychology and attention to the ideological purposes of the discipline. Both routes involve abandoning psychology's role in supporting the modernist quest for certainty in a world of frag-mentation and shifting complexities. The first possibility available to the critical psychologist is postmodern playfulness. The second is an exploration of an interpretative and culturally embedded psychology.

Postmodern critiques of psychology and their relation to teacher education

'Postmodern' is itself a problematic term when used in relation to psychology. It was suggested earlier that psychology became positioned by policy-makers as a cure for the fragmentation and uncertainties of the modern world. It was the pessimism and alienation from the pro-gressivism associated with commercialism and twentieth-century capit-alism found in the visions of modernity represented by, for example, modernist writers such as Eliot, Pound and Kafka which produced fertile ground for the development of psychology. While Freud's work gave validity to the crises of subjectivity and representation experienced by self-aware liberals, the more mainstream work of experimental psychologists, outlined earlier, attempted to assist modernizing govern-ments to place order on disorder. Education, doubtless owing to its function as maker of citizens, has found itself the site of battle between the ideologies informed by these competing versions of psychology. Of these, no site was probably more public than the attempts made at the promotion of progressive versions of primary education by some educationists in England in the late 1960s and early 1970s. Though, as both Riley (1983) and Walkerdine (1984) have suggested, Freudian psychology, which influenced progressive education via Melanie Klein and Susan Isaacs, also served a normalizing function of social control once it was inserted into early educational contexts.

So what can a postmodern critique of psychology and hence the way it supports specific forms of state-funded education offer education? If the modernist critique searches for a way out of the alienation of modernity, some versions of postmodern analysis, suspicious of grand narratives, do not seek grand solutions but playfully and mockingly slide across the surfaces of the human condition destabilizing the assumptions that sustain current ideologies. But how helpful is this for education? It has been suggested elsewhere (Edwards and Knight, 1994) that in the UK academics' preoccupation with postmodernism was perhaps the chattering classes' great gift to Thatcherism, preventing any robust and principled defence of the education system being dismantled during the 1980s. Kvale's description of postmodern thought catches these concerns:

> Postmodern thought focuses on the surface, with a refined sensibility to what appears, a differentiation of what is perceived. The relation of sign and signifier is breaking down: the reference to a reality beyond the sign recedes. In the media, texts and images refer less to an external world beyond the signs than to a chain of signifiers, to other texts and images . . . The image, the appearance is everything; the appearance has become the essence.
> (Kvale, 1992: 37–8)

The decentred postmodern version of selfhood, connecting to, or ironically distancing from, the images presented to it, does not look beyond the representation to seek motives and meanings. In these terms education may be the delivered curriculum presented attractively. It may be accepted unquestioningly or mocked playfully while other images grab attention. The decentred self does not possess the individual identity project (Luckmann, 1982) which gave personal purpose to engagement with the world. Cleverness rather than engagement assists the glide of refined sensibility across the surfaces of understanding.

A postmodern critique may destabilize the power of the assumptions through which ideologies shape individual's interpretations of their worlds. Indeed Gergen argues that the postmodern turn allows a critical eye to be placed on the disciplinary assumptions of psychology such as beliefs in a basic subject matter, universal properties, empirical methods and research as progressive (Gergen, 1992). But science, and hence scientific versions of psychology, with its current social representation as modern rationality (Moscovici, 1998) is firmly embedded in the western mind as that which saves us from, for example, authoritarian irrationality. The neutrality of science sits alongside the neutrality of government, judicial systems and perpetrators of 'just wars'. We see science invoked by participants on both sides of debates about genetically modified food, the teaching of reading and ways of measuring school improvement. The certainty of science is hard to shift.

The pinpricks of postmodern critiques, however, reach only surface representations and do not seem to engage, for example, with the processes of the social formation of mind, the opportunities and constraints available in educational systems and how they are discussed. If psychology is to grapple with these issues, a retreat into playful versions of postmodern critique is not helpful. It is not enough, for example, to emphasize the paradoxes and discontinuities of knowledge in action. It is an important step to do so, but an insufficient one. A critique of psychology and its uses within education therefore needs to address quite explicitly relationships between knowledge, culture, mind and action and perhaps begin to identify possibilities for life-enhancing actions.

The distinctions within critical psychology between postmodernism and social constructivism are, however, not always clear cut and are frequently and confusingly used interchangeably (Fox and Prilleltensky, 1997). There are similarities. Both engage with the discursive construction of self or selves and both sustain an attack on narrow foundationalism in the human sciences. Both explore how knowledge existing in cultures speaks through individuals as they act in those cultures. Both value the knowledge that is generated in interactions in knowledge communities by the participants in the practices of the communities, over that produced by the academy. Both would seem to call for that form of educational knowledge which emphasizes knowing *that* over knowing *why*. But they explore these issues at slightly different levels of gaze and for different reasons.

The postmodern turn, evidenced first in analyses of knowledge and society (Seidman, 1994), has led to critical analyses of individuals' sense-making through examination of their discursive strategies (D. Edwards, 1997) and hence their positioning within their knowledge communities (see, for example, A. Edwards, 1997a, on how student teachers are positioned as learners in classrooms). The gaze of postmodern criticism has been from the social to the individual, and in a celebration of relativism it has not sought to explain the patterns it observes and unsettles. Social constructivism, however, with its roots in those forms of developmental and social psychology which are crucially conscious of how the mind is socially formed, places its gaze on the processes of social formation of mind. Social constructivism has flourished in a climate made possible by the challenges to the enlightenment offered by postmodern critiques, but arguably offers explanations for the formation of mind more readily than it attempts the social critique.

The distinctions are important in relation to teacher training and explorations of how people learn. Critique, self-awareness and the tentative testing of meanings in action are prerequisites for social sciences which purport to be more than modernist constructions but can offer insights of value to practitioners in their fields of practice. The postmodern turn has allowed us to begin to reconceptualize relations between knowledge and practice and to move on from the sterile and futile dualism of the application of knowledge to practice. However, a concern with the professional development of teachers has to take us to a focus on how teachers construct and use knowledge in practice. It requires a gaze that is fixed on the sense-making and actions of practitioners so that we may understand how that sense-making may be usefully informed, and in turn itself inform professional understanding.

An interpretative psychology and theorizing teachers

Discussion of teaching as informed decision-making leads us to seek an interpretative psychology which can inform and support teachers' theorizing. An interpretative – or hermeneutic – psychology may be particularly useful when considering professional practice as the use of existing competences to meet professional goals that have been identified by the actor. Here we return to the description, earlier in this chapter, of teaching as skilful interpretations of learners and the contexts of learning and the careful negotiations of possible meanings with those learners. An interpretative psychology in use in teaching would sustain a capacity to 'read' situations, a disposition to do so and the availability of those intellectual and social resources which would make worthwhile responses possible.

An interpretative psychology which informs teachers' selections of responses to learners is not an atheoretical individualized psychology but one which offers practitioners insights into the interpretations they make and the responses they have available. Taylor's argument for 'peaceful coexistence in psychology' (Taylor, 1985: 117ff) carefully distinguishes between a classical model of psychology which serves a purpose but relies on the use of 'brute data', i.e. data which are not interpreted by the observer, and a hermeneutic version which is no less interested in causal relationships between acts and outcomes but which connects them through informed interpretations of meanings, motivations and intentions. The latter version of psychology, he suggests, is well suited to theories of learning.

An interpretative psychology therefore might be a resource for teachers as they theorize, by validating both their searches for meaning in complex contexts and their own capacity to select appropriate responses. In searching for meaning teachers are arguably assisted by what Vygotsky (1987) described as 'scientific concepts' which are different from the everyday concepts which guide the thinking of those whom Brown *et al.* (1989) have called 'just plain folks'. Vygotsky's scientific concepts are rooted in the world as currently understood, anchored in theory and made disembedded thinking possible. Vygotsky's emphasis on scientific concepts as 'tools' with which we can test the world and which in turn we test in the world would seem to underpin any notion of the theorizing teacher. Theorizing teachers and learners are, in such a version of learning, actively seeking meaning as they move from the familiar to the less familiar (Greeno, 1997).

But this version of psychology, by making considerable demands on teachers, requires an enhanced version of the responsible agency of teachers as professionals. The similarities between the concerns of postmodern and social constructivist analyses listed in the previous section of this chapter would seem to have much in common with those recently modernized teacher training strategies which emphasize individual performativity and the death of the foundation subjects. But here we touch on a tension for those governments which have promoted school-based teacher training and notions of teachers' craft knowledge as elements in their attempts to control teacher training.

Removing initial teacher training from the power of the universities, while heavily regulating what influence remains with university tutors, does not necessarily make the training easier to control. For example, local knowledge, constructed and used in local knowledge communities, can assume a life of its own unless the options for action available in the sites of knowledge construction are regulated. In England the regulation of classroom teaching is evident through inspection processes, national curricula, frequent national assessments, target setting for pupil performance, systems of long- and short-term planning for curriculum delivery, prescribed pedagogies for the teaching of literacy and numeracy and performance-related pay. Student teachers are inducted into these systems through a system of training which hinges on observations made by their teacher mentors of their individual performances against the carefully timed plans they prepare prior to each session.

The isolation of student teachers, their reliance on the state-approved targets and planning mechanisms in these heavily regulated environments reduces the influences on student teachers' identity

formation that might be offered by more expert teachers, local education authorities, subject associations etc. The language-games currently
available to beginning teachers as learners are geared to the demonstra-
tion of individual performance against government targets.

Student teachers' relative isolation while learning to teach in schools
has been examined recently in a series of studies (Edwards and Collison,
1996; Edwards and Ogden, 1998a, 1998b; 1999a, 1999b). There it was
argued that the potential that school-based teacher training holds for
student teachers' learning through participation in a professional community of practice was in part being undermined by an underdeveloped
notion of mentoring and school-based training. Current versions of
mentoring appear to sustain a view that learning to teach is the application of curricular knowledge in classrooms and that a mentoring
system should be based on monitoring by mentors rather than model-
ling (Edwards and Ogden, 1998b). Importantly, mentoring and school-
based training lack a discourse in which student teachers might be
positioned as legitimate learners (Edwards and Collison, 1996; Edwards,
1997a). The studies have led to the conclusion that English teacher
training is currently likely to create practitioners who have been trained
in performativity against externally derived criteria rather than intelligently interpreting professional decision-makers able to respond to
pupils as learners (Edwards, 1998; 2001).

It seems that the mechanisms of the modernizing state are successfully impeding the impact of the postmodern turn on initial teacher
training. Schools are not being developed as local sites in which professional knowledge, as sets of grounded, theoretically anchored and constantly tested scientific concepts, can be used by theorizing teachers.
Consequently student teachers are not being inducted as responsible
agents through sets of experiences which encourage them to learn
how to interpret classrooms and respond to what they discern. The
teachers who are being socially constructed in teacher training are
likely to become expert in the following of predetermined lesson
plans (Edwards and Ogden, 1998a). The trust that brings some cohesion
to the shifting uncertainties of modernity (Bauman, 1993; Giddens,
1990; Kvale, 1992) seems to be vigorously denied teachers as they
work with both student teachers and pupils. And deprofessionalization
is the outcome.

Psychology has shown little interest in supporting teachers' professionalism. As the academic discipline safeguarded by the American
Psychological Association, the Australian Psychological Society and
the British Psychological Society it has been appropriated to and there-

fore adapted to the modernizing agenda of governments. Instead of operating as an engaged social science, which develops through responding to issues of practice, being self-critically aware of policy imperatives and responsibly informing teaching to enhance learning, the academic version of psychology has, in the most part, remained distanced and disengaged from the intentional actions of those it persists in labelling its 'subjects'. Consequently this version of psychology has served teacher training and teachers poorly.

Yet teaching, if it purports to be a profession endowed with the trust afforded professionals (at least until recently), has to be informed by more than its own historical craft-based practices and government directives. The paucity of its knowledge-base is evident when one attempts to analyse education as the disciplinary base of pedagogical decision-making using Schwab's categories of substantive and syntactic knowledge (Westbury and Wilkof, 1978). Currently the substantive knowledge (the *what* of educational knowledge) in England appears to reside largely in knowledge of the curriculum as sets of teaching targets enriched by the pedagogical knowledge licensed increasingly overtly by government guidelines. The syntactic knowledge of education (i.e. *ways of knowing* and talking about education) as a body of knowledge informing professional practice, is in its most limited form simply that which is prescribed in the quality assurance systems of the national inspection system. Meanwhile in its least restricted form most commonly discussed, it is a capacity to reflect upon and discuss one's practice. The theorizing teacher drawing on and informing an educational knowledge-base consisting of Vygotskian-style 'scientific concepts' of, for example, pedagogy is not the most ubiquitous image of the teacher-practitioner.

The vacuum in specialized educational knowledge just outlined is perhaps unsurprising. Education in the UK has been a battleground. One battle relevant here was between the foundation disciplines, where psychology seemed to be firmly trounced by sociology in the late 1970s. That skirmish was quickly followed by a longer war of attrition between government and the universities, whose hold on teacher training was weakened by a series of reforms in the early 1990s which placed initial training more firmly in school settings where craft knowledge could be acquired. Resistance to their fate by the foundation disciplines during the 1980s was difficult for two reasons. First, there was little worth defending in the psychology offered to student teachers during initial training in the 1970s. It predated the development of social constructivism in psychology and all too frequently was presented as a body of accumulated knowledge, not always directly relevant to education, that claimed to have universal applications; and only too rarely as a way of informing the interpretations and professional responses of teachers. Second, there was surprisingly little history of interdisciplinarity in education. Sociology and psychology, the two dominant disciplines in the 1970s, were so epistemologically opposed that collaboration, either for mutual defence or for creative repositioning, appeared a non-starter.

The situation is different at the beginning of a new century. The blurring of disciplinary boundaries highlighted in the postmodern turn is commonplace. For example, multidisciplinarity, evidenced as the capacity to work at the margins of disciplinary knowledge in order to meet the current and future challenges presented by society, is a funding priority for the UK research councils. Working at the boundaries applies also to the restructuring of professional practices in healthcare settings (Engeström, 1993), combining disparate practices to create new forms of practice such as educare (Anning and Edwards, 1999) and rethinking relationships between knowledge created in practice and academe (Gibbons *et al.*, 1994). A knowledge-base for education, which is constantly informed and reformed by work carried out by educationally grounded forms of social science, which responsibly engage together in supporting and informing the generation of locally relevant knowledge in the actions of knowledgeable teachers, might be a timely aim.

Chapter 6

Collaborative responses to uncertainty

In this chapter we ask 'how might teacher education respond to the need to create learners able to generate as well as use knowledge?' Ensuring that teaching is not limited to promoting passive regurgitation calls for informed responsible teachers, who are able to make choices when helping learners to use the resources available to them. It demands a capacity to work with rather than avoid uncertainty. We suggest that it demands theorizing teachers able to take deliberative action. Specific challenges therefore face initial training and continuing professional development. We answer our question by invoking sociocultural interpretations of teaching and learning which see relationships between learners, teachers, knowledge and contexts as a dynamic weaving together of opportunities and constraints which shape both teaching and learning.

What kinds of teachers for what kinds of learners?

Do you know the story about the time machine? In 1900 it collected a surgeon and a teacher and set them down in 2000 in, respectively, an operating theatre and a classroom. The surgeon was bewildered by the new environment. The teacher picked up some chalk and carried on with the lesson. If there is a crisis in education, it is that it has adapted so little to the society produced by late capitalism. It is a triumph of conservatism that curriculum is so often distinctly different from both the knowledge that children bring to school and from that which they will use when they leave it; that passive regurgitation is prized over a disposition to enquire; and that teachers are assessed on their ability to deliver knowledge rather than to assure understanding and support children's dispositions to be learners. A system which can be justified only as a mechanism for social control has been in part shored up by those aspects of psychology which, as we argued in the last chapter, are driven by their own insecurities.

It is surely timely to ask the following questions. What kinds of learners are we likely to need? What kinds of pedagogical practices are likely to support their learning? What kinds of teachers do we think will be able to offer such support? Where are these teachers and how are they to be supported? These are not modernist 'clean slate' questions (Toulmin, 1990, and Chapter 4 above). They are more in tune with Kozulin's notion of 'a return to the beginning' (Kozulin, 1996: 161) where, in explaining the need for a prospective rather than a retrospective education, he points to weaknesses in cumulative versions of science which see earlier work merely as weaker approximations of current certainties. Instead, he suggests, we need to look to literature where, for example, Plato, Shakespeare, Hegel and Tolstoy do not represent traditions which are reducible to each other, rather they are 'different attempts to solve the same set of fundamental problems' (p. 161). Kozulin is signalling that we need to return to the problems rather than simply compare existing solutions, return to the beginning, rather than see progress simply in terms of a process in which our knowledge is refined through successive accumulation.

Such a return to the beginning has implications both for how learners are positioned in current models of teaching and learning and for how education professionals use the knowledge available to them. For learners, an emphasis on learning as authoring understandings renders difficult any notion of learning as simply reproduction. Meanwhile education professionals are licensed, by Kozulin's advice, to revisit quite basic questions and draw on recent knowledge only if it assists in solving current preparations for future developments. Building education policies entirely on notions of current accumulations of knowledge identified as 'what works' can result in these policies being retrospective rather than prospective. Kozulin's suggestion, that we return to the beginning, reminds us that what education needs is a form of professional practice which is driven by the authoring of effective pedagogy by professionals who are informed by and inform a shared understanding of pedagogies which meet the current and foreseeable needs of learners and their worlds. The collusion of some versions of psychology in a retrospective focus was discussed in the previous chapter. There it was argued that academic psychology's focus on accumulating knowledge about discrete areas of human functioning has led to a fragmented knowledge-base and a preoccupation with maintaining existing fields of study within the discipline.

Shotter makes a similar point in his analysis of psychology as a discipline which limits itself to justifying the claims to knowledge that are made. He is particularly concerned by the discipline's insensitivity to persons as agents with their own purposes. In response, he suggests that psychology should broaden its aims in order to tackle problems 'of an ontological kind' (Shotter, 1993: 148) and 'respect the being' (p. 149) of persons. Shotter's psychology is a responsive and responsible social science which engages with the concerns of people as responsible agents acting with deliberation in the world, and it is a version of psychology which will be explored in this chapter in relation to teacher education. In the terms set out in Chapter 3 above this version of psychology disrupts the protective belt around the core of the discipline to question some quite fundamental assumptions about psychology, its methodology and its purposes.

Agentic teachers

Charles Taylor, teasing out what marks being a person means, rather than being an animal or even a machine, lights on humans' capacity to respond to what is significant to them in events. To that attribute he adds a sensitivity to certain goals or standards which, because each person represents them in order to consider them, are constituted for an individual in a personal way (Taylor, 1985). This is an individualistic constructivist version of being an interpreting and reinterpreting person and it suggests that education policies which rely on an easily transferable knowledge-base are mistaken. Educational knowledge is unlikely to be used in predictable ways by practitioners. As Billig points out, even bureaucrats bend and create rules in ways that suggest that they are adapting their behaviours in interaction with others (Billig, 1987). Interpreting and responsive teachers, at the very least, construct their own understandings of classrooms and try to respond to what they regard to be important within them. Their agency, or capacity for individual responsible action, lies in the extent to which they are able to interpret and respond in ways which ensure they are dealing with what is significant for them. In situations where teachers' actions are heavily circumscribed, their agency is restricted.

Yet the emphasis on individual and personal sense-making offered so far is a limited notion of agency. Taylor later argues (Taylor, 1991) that it is a potentially dangerous form of self-fashioning which, as presented here, can appear to ignore a system of common values and shared commitment to socially oriented goals constructed within and sustained by the social practices of the communities in which we participate.

Shotter covers similar ground, arguing that psychology has for too long concerned itself more with causal than with ethical questions (Shotter, 1993) and in doing so has paid insufficient attention to the dialogic formation of moral and social responsibility. An emphasis on the dialogic processes underpinning understandings of social responsibility also resonates with Benhabib's arguments for an interactive rationality (Benhabib, 1992).

Benhabib's thesis, that the certainty of authoritative claims to rationality needs to be replaced by a discursive rationality, is an important attempt to see agency as socially responsible. Her responsibly engaged agent is capable of flexible yet morally grounded adaptation to the shifting demands of postmodernity. Her 'situated self', connected to its community and its values, is not a retreat to relativism but an attempt to reconfigure universalism by situating it in moral conversations in which the capacity to see the other's point of view is of paramount importance. Her argument positions active agency quite centrally and in doing so allows us to distinguish her view of agency from both experimental psychology's idea of agent as an object to be manipulated and from the denial of purposive agency by some versions of postmodernism. At the same time, her attention to the discursive practices, which are in part captured by the language-games outlined in Chapter 3 above, and which offer validity to constructions of the world, supports our shift of focus towards learning as self-authored knowledge production.

Shotter's causal-ethical distinction and Benhabib's alternative construction of moral responsibility helpfully highlight two of the themes of modernizing governments and remind us of the extent to which central control has gained ground in the moral as well as intellectual spheres of teachers' actions. We have already argued that over the last few decades education can be seen as a battleground on which modernizing governments have attempted to stake out what the values and socially oriented goals of education should be. Their opponents, emerging from the specialist communities of, for example, teachers of English, teacher education and educational research, have done no more than offer short-lived defences, usually unassisted by neighbouring communities. Far from being sets of self-authoring professionals, defining their own agency and the values that inform it, teachers and teacher educators have been fashioned as individual professionals whose relationship with the state has become what Seddon describes as 'learned occupational helplessness' (Seddon, 1999: 3).

The spaces for the exercise of responsible agency have been dramatically reduced through the state's interventions in curricula, in its control of quality assurance systems and, in England and parts of the USA, in definitions of appropriate pedagogical practices in core areas of the curriculum. Worryingly, restrictions on the exercise of teacher agency have the potential to lead to an emphasis on curriculum delivery at the expense of responsive and interactive pedagogy. Tochon and Munby (1993) draw a distinction between teaching which operates with a diachronic, i.e. linear, time epistemology and teaching where there is a synchronic approach to time which allows connections to be made between learner and curriculum, in the moment. The former they associate with didactics in the mainland Europe sense of curriculum planning and delivery, and the latter with what they describe as a capacity to operate pedagogically and responsively. Their analysis suggests that a reliance on diachronic teaching is more evident among less experienced practitioners and evidence of synchronic action among the more experienced. Synchronic teaching importantly presupposes that teachers are interpreting agents with the professional freedom to respond knowledgeably in a deliberative way to learners' pedagogic needs.

Tochon and Munby's analysis raises questions about how novice teachers are helped to become the kinds of practitioners needed to help learners to develop dispositions to engage with and learn from the opportunities available to them. A recent exploration of how student teachers in England learn to respond to pupils as learners has shown that teacher training programmes emphasize the individual performance of student teachers. The result of this is that student teachers operate in isolation from their co-operating teachers (mentors in the UK), follow their lesson plans as activity scripts and are inhibited in their responsive interactions with pupils. For example, student teachers apologize for deviating from their lesson plans in order to answer unanticipated questions from pupils. One conclusion from this study was that student teachers were being trained to become self-monitoring deliverers of an agreed curriculum (Edwards and Ogden, 1998a). And, far from being trained to interpret and respond to pupils' needs, the emphasis placed on their need to deliver their plans meant that they actually avoided risky pedagogic interactions (Edwards, 1998; Edwards and Ogden, 1999a). These analyses located the focus on pre-scripted student teacher performance in the heavy quality-assurance mechanisms which control the initial teacher training curriculum and its 'delivery' in England. The reference to the dangers of 'personally-arrived at pedagogies' made by the then Head of the English Teacher Training Agency and discussed in the previous chapter (Millett, 1996) signalled clearly that an erosion of professional agency in pedagogy was on the agenda. It now seems that this agenda is being played out in teacher education in England.

But how has this agenda been so successfully realized? Part of the reason for weak versions of teacher professionalism must lie in the extent to which responses to restrictions on it have been largely limited to spirited defences of traditional representations of teachers as individual professional decision-makers. Responses have not sufficiently considered the extent to which professional agency is socially constructed through participation in professional communities of practice – or, in Benhabib's terms, is situated in communities and constituted and renewed through the processes of discursive rationality (Benhabib, 1992). Elliott's reminder to action researchers of the opportunities for professional growth to be found in collaborative action research which 'involves the restructuring of practical consciousness through the reconstruction of their store of mutual knowledge' (Elliott, 1993: 184) similarly points to the potential inherent in discursive consciousness and at the same time connects agency to professional learning as a collaborative enterprise.

Learning as increasingly informed participation

In the previous section a distinction was made between versions of agency which focus on individuality and versions which emphasize its relationship to the moral purposes of social worlds. This distinction will also underlie discussion of teachers' professional learning. So far in this chapter, a particular version of teachers as professionals has been suggested. This version sees teachers as self-authoring members of communities of practice whose sense of moral purpose as professionals is developed in responsible interactions with others. The version of agency proposed is therefore a relational agency. In addition, there have been hints that teachers' professional action can be described more as ways of *being*, *seeing* and *responding* in classrooms than simply in terms of the application of knowledge, however powerful the warrants accorded to that knowledge. Learning, therefore, is as much a question of personal transformation (Moll and Greenberg, 1990) as it is increased familiarity with scientific concepts of pedagogy and their relevance. Indeed the two elements are intertwined, as personal transformation is seen in changes in how situations are interpreted and responded to.

This summary recognizes that learning, interpreting and responding manifest themselves differently in different individuals, but that the processes which support a developing expertise are embedded in social practices. Before moving on to Kozulin's type of basic question (Kozulin, 1996) in order to ask what kind of teacher education for what kind of teacher, the view of learning alluded to requires some unpacking. A brief outline is sketched in Table 4. These definitions are as applicable to the learning of a novice teacher as they are to a four-year-old who is starting school. They draw on sociocultural and activity theory interpretations of practices (Chaiklin and Lave, 1993; Engeström, 1999; Lave and Wenger, 1991; Resnick *et al.*, 1991; Wertsch, 1985, 1991; Wertsch *et al.*, 1995) and are located within a research tradition which originated in the work of Vygotsky.

Table 4 Features of a sociocultural pedagogy

A sociocultural pedagogy sees	*learning* as increasingly informed participation in the practices of a community.
	learners as people who are acquiring new ways of interpreting and responding to their environment.
	knowledge as something recognized, acquired and also generated through participating in the practices of a community.
	a community as a set of practices e.g. a mathematics community, a professional community of elementary teaching.
	teachers as those who assist the interpretations and responses of learners, for example, by modelling, explaining and manipulating the environment.
	pedagogical practice as a process of making judgements about the strategies to be used to assist learners' increasingly informed interpretations and responses.
	learning environments as sets of opportunities for participation which may provide varying degrees of freedom of action.

A sociocultural pedagogy therefore aims at assisting learners' participation in communities where knowledge is used and constructed. Greeno, for example describes learning as the increasingly effective participation of an individual in the activities of a system (Greeno, 1997). The influence of cognitive anthropologists such as Lave (1988) and Scribner (1985) on this explanation of learning explains its focus on how learners are inducted into *existing* practices and helped to see the opportunities for action that are recognized as available by current members of the community. Indeed Cole talks of how 'the cultural past is reified in the cultural present in the forms of the artifacts that mediate the process of co-construction' (Cole, 1995: 193). Sociocultural psychology can therefore be seen to be retrospective and well suited to the sharing of existing knowledge. However, we shall argue later that it does offer a framework for learning in formal settings where the aim is to produce as well as use knowledge. But we turn first to explanations of acting (in which we include thinking) and the model of mind which underpins understandings of learning as increasingly informed participation.

The participation metaphor for learning presupposes that our learning is supported by our interactions with our environment and that our thinking is shaped by these interactions. Here we enter the language-game of distributed cognitions and intelligences. The argument that cognitions are distributed within contexts and activities offers a considerable challenge to those models of mind that lead us to talk about knowledge being acquired, stockpiled and then applied. It quite radically questions those filing-cabinet metaphors of cognition which see it as simply the storing of representations which we can call up when we need them. Instead, situated cognition locates cognitive processes in the actions provoked by the activity in context (Lave, 1988). Following this line, Brown *et al.* (1989) argue that thought and action are shaped, or scaffolded, by the possibilities inherent in an activity in its current social context.

But these are not simple determinist assertions claiming that our minds are merely shaped by our environments. The argument is far more subtle. One element of the argument is that learning is a matter of interpreting our worlds in progressively more complex ways and acquiring the capacity for increasingly effective responses. But of course contexts and activities will vary in the interpretations allowed and responses permitted. And, as Valsiner points out, the degrees of freedom we have for interpretation and response within a learning zone can vary to shape our learning in quite different ways (Valsiner, 1998).

A particular take on how support for learning is distributed across learning environments is offered by Pea (Pea, 1993). He talks of intelligence as a resource to be used, which is distributed across people, artefacts and other environmental features and which can support our responses. In Pea's analysis intelligence is therefore something to be 'accomplished rather than possessed' (p. 50). Much therefore depends on our capacity to see the potential for action within a context. The situationalist view is that the processes of learning are an enhanced engagement with the resources for sense-making and action that are available within a setting. Learning is not so much an accumulation of knowledge as a reorientation to knowledge as both a user and producer of knowledge within a set of social practices. Such a reorientation involves an improved capacity to recognize the intelligence, i.e. the resources that might scaffold performance, that are available in a setting.

The importance situationalists place on recognition suggests that one of the roles of the teacher is to assist the learner at the point of interpretation of the activity and its knowledge practices and at the point of response to these interpretations. Drawing on Gibson's ecological idea of the affordances available in a particular niche (i.e. what permissible behaviours a person's surroundings afford – Gibson, 1979), we might argue that teachers need to assist learners' searches for the affordances for action available to them when they encounter new challenges. Meanwhile, simultaneously, they need to be aware of how these searches are constrained by learners' capacities to recognize the potential for action available to them (Ellis, 1997; Anning and Edwards, 1999). Learners' successful use of the affordances available to them helps them to build both the capacity to interpret the affordance and the ability to use it into their repertoires of interpretations and responses. In the case of student teachers, the repertoire to be developed centres on pedagogic actions.

For example, a student teacher's recognition that children are out of their seats sharpening pencils, exchanging erasers etc. because the academic tasks of the classroom are poorly pitched is part of a process of developing skilful pattern recognition to enable the beginning teacher to distinguish between acceptable and unacceptable off-task behaviour. When the diagnosis is followed by a successful decision to alter the pace of the activity or to provide additional scaffolding, e.g. extra resources or additional explanations, the student teacher is building up a repertoire of responses to recognizable patterns of pupil behaviour. The niche of the classroom in that example offers a range of affordances for teachers as possibilities for action. These include continuous nagging at pupils to return to the task or a complete change of task for the whole class, as well as the more pedagogical solution just outlined. But the pedagogical response can be invoked only if the diagnosis allows that set of affordances to be an option, i.e. the problem is diagnosed as a pedagogical one rather than one of poor behaviour.

This example raises a number of questions about the nature of supervision and feedback commonly offered in initial training to student teachers by their school-based mentors. Our argument is that learning to teach is a question of building up a repertoire of increasingly informed interpretations of affordances, and responses which make use of those affordances *in the act of teaching*. It would seem, therefore, that student teachers, as learners, would best be supported by supervising experts who model, guide, enhance and even challenge student teachers' interpretations and responses while teaching. Co-teaching with mentors would appear to be a sensible way of enhancing student teachers' learning. The common practice of observation and feedback which mentors are usually encouraged to undertake seems to miss an opportunity for supporting the informed participation of student teachers in the community of practice of teaching. Indeed, observation and feedback frequently operate as a system for monitoring the extent to which student teachers have adhered to their lesson plans and have not been distracted by unanticipated pupil needs. Recognizing these pupil needs would demand that student teachers deviate from their plans for curriculum delivery and explore the affordances for pedagogic action available to them.

Building up patterns of recognition and response, which are continuously field-tested and refined, is an important feature of learning for those who see learning as heavily situated in local affordances. Greeno even explains transfer of understanding from one context to another (the bugbear of situationalists) as a 'generality of knowing' seen in the patterns of participation evident in someone's interactions (Greeno, 1997). Clearly Greeno, like most situationalists, has not abandoned the idea that the mind processes information, but instead argues that the relationship between mind and environment is more complex than a simple information-processing model of mind allows for (Anderson *et al.*, 2000; Sfard, 1998).

As we can see from the meaning given to the term 'cognition', the language-game in which we find talk of distributed cognitions is different from the game in which we speak of mind as a store of knowledge to be applied. But we would caution against too extreme a notion of distribution of cognition. Like Salomon we find the 'the idea . . . novel and provocative. However it can be carried too far' (Salomon, 1993: 111). Instead, we would argue that it is fruitful to go as far as to acknowledge that the filing-cabinet metaphor of mind as a system of well-organized knowledge applied reflectively in action has not proved entirely useful. It underpinned those pre-reform models of teacher training in England which were based on the application, in schools, of knowledge acquired in universities, by student teachers. It was rightly dismissed as ineffective. However, the model we are suggesting here, i.e. that of a situated mind engaged in a process of interpreting and reinterpreting its relationship with the knowledge available to it in its ecological niche, is a complex model. The mind may not be a filing cabinet in this new model, but neither is it activated only by external cues. What is being learnt when we tackle something novel can be seen to exist both in the context and in the constructs we bring to our explorations of the context. This less extreme version of distributed cognitions therefore does not rule out the need for access to some features of knowledge through more formal methods of knowledge transmission.

Interestingly, it is to robotics that we turn for an interpreting model of mind which offers support for the thesis that successful learning involves increasingly informed interpretations of opportunities for action and a developing capacity to respond to them. Clark describes the new science of the connectionist mind as a 'cognitive science of the embodied mind' (Clark, 1997: xiii). He characterizes the shift it announces as a move from seeing the mind as a repository of encoded representations, and a mechanism whose strength is demonstrated in the detail of its inner organization, to seeing it as a 'locus of inner *structures* that act as operators on the world via their role in determining actions' (Clark, 1997: 47). In crude summary, the mind that Clark describes interprets and responds to the contexts of actions and exploits the affordances for effective action within them. Clark's connectionist mind is an outward-looking mind, which seeks local scaffolding, which might enhance purposive action. In summary, the connectionist model of mind that Clark describes can be compared with the more traditional information-processing or filing-cabinet model of mind as in Table 5.

So what are the implications of the connectionist mind for, first, the education of children in school and, second, for the training of those who are to teach them? The first point to note is that the connectionist mind appears to meet a concern with developing learners' dispositions

Table 5 A comparison of information-processing and connectionist models of mind

Information-processing model of mind	Connectionist model of mind
• The mind is a system of stored facts etc. which we can call upon to solve problems.	• The mind is a mechanism for interpreting the potential for action available in the environment.
• The main function of the mind is therefore to encode the information that it meets and store it efficiently.	• The main function of the mind is to decode the environment to assist the selection of worthwhile responses.
• Mind, body, and environment need to be considered as separate system.	• Mind is embodied and learns how to interpret specific types of environment.
• Knowledge is carried in the mind and is context-free.	• Mind is primed to look for familiar patterns when it moves to a new environment and tries to interpret it.
• Learning is a question of efficient knowledge acquisition.	• Learning is therefore heavily dependent on contextual cues.

to engage flexibly with the shifting challenges of postmodernity. But it also makes specific demands on teachers as they deal with complexity. These demands include the need to attend to:

- learners' dispositions to engage with new experiences
- how they might help learners interpret new experiences and respond to them
- the ways of interpreting experiences that learners bring with them from home and other settings
- how adults work together co-operatively to support learners' increasingly informed participation in the practices of, for example, science
- how that participation is monitored
- how to structure environments in order to support specific kinds of participation
- how to use the resources available to respond to pupils' pedagogic needs
- the learning potential in learner-led activities.

It calls, therefore, for an interventionist pedagogy which is in tune with UK governments' interventionist preoccupation with social investment for economic inclusion (Giddens, 1998). But interventions in this pedagogy occur in and while building on pupils' current experience in order to augment the experience, and not through the delivery of parcels of knowledge. It is a pedagogy which acknowledges Vygotsky's dictum that learning occurs on two planes, first on the social or intermental plane and then on the more personal or intramental plane. It is also a pedagogy which acknowledges learners as producers of knowledge by recognizing the contributions to local knowledge that might be made by learners when they bring their own knowledge into play.

It is a pedagogy which finds support in Scardamalia and Bereiter's description of knowledge-building communities and a knowledge-building pedagogy (Scardamalia and Bereiter, 1999). They argue that children who are being prepared to participate in a knowledge economy which sees knowledge as products which can be sold, refined, discarded etc. need an education which prepares them for knowledge-production and contributing to the knowledge economy. They do not dismiss education that focuses on acquiring content knowledge, but suggest that pupils need both sets of experience. They are not advocating another version of discovery learning. Rather learners are encouraged to see themselves as cognitive apprentices who are learning to think and act as young scientists etc. The knowledge they produce is unlikely to be new knowledge, but it will be new to them. And attention is placed primarily on the processes of knowledge-production and a developing capacity to use the resources available to them, i.e. to use the affordances in the situation, in solving knowledge problems. In a UK study with early years workers, using a similar focus on authentic ways of thinking and acting, children as young as three were encouraged through role play and careful resourcing to think and act, for example mathematically, while 'being' engineers who build boats (Anning and Edwards, 1999).

It is a pedagogy which requires theorizing teachers able to attend to the complexity we have just outlined. It is a pedagogy which is hard to train for. Training for this interactive interpretative pedagogy cannot be based simply on sending novice practitioners into classrooms with lesson plans and seeing how well they deliver them. An interpretative, knowledge-building pedagogy requires a version of training that sees classroom teaching as a community of practice in which novices participate in increasingly informed ways alongside more expert practitioners who help them interpret and respond to classroom events by sharing with novices the lenses of expertise they employ in their interpretations. It is a model which also requires an understanding of classrooms as places where practitioners are knowledge-builders and where discursive problem-solving is a legitimate activity which supports deliberative professional action.

This is a very different model of training from that which operates in England. There it is commonplace for mentors to divide their classes so that student teachers teach one or two groups while the mentors focus on the remaining pupils; or for the mentors to leave the classrooms and the student teachers alone and in charge; or for the mentors to observe the students while student teachers teach and subsequently receive formal feedback. In an early, but extensive, study of school-based initial teacher training in elementary schools we found very few examples of co-teaching where mentors and student teachers worked together so that mentors could share their interpretations of events and explain their responses in the moment of the pedagogical interactions (Edwards and Collison, 1996). In the same study, using a Bakhtinian notion of addressivity to explore the self-positioning of student teachers in conversations with their mentors, we found that knowledge-building conversations between teacher-mentors and student teachers were not warranted by the cultures of classrooms, where the pupils were the only legitimate learners (Edwards, 1997a). A more recent study, which focused explicitly on how student teachers learn to interpret pupils' pedagogical needs, has come to the same conclusion and, in addition, is noting that the feedback conversations provided do not assist student teachers' capacity for interpretations of classroom events (Edwards and Ogden, 1998b; 1999a). A connectionist model of mind coupled with an understanding of learning as increasingly informed participation may, perhaps, provide stimuli for rethinking both initial and continuing teacher education and the relationships within them.

Changing practices in teacher education

Pedagogical practices in the more affluent parts of the world are bound to change, if only because how we position ourselves in relation to knowledge is changing. In societies where young children are competent internet users and the workplace is typified by series of individual desks where workers manage projects using a range of research and communication skills, biscuit-factory models of education already appear anachronistic. Current policy responses to the demands of the knowledge economy appear, however, to operate with an information-processing model of mind which emphasizes curriculum coverage and a focus on transferring to new contexts technical practices that 'work'. While we do not wish to deny that access to public knowledge is essential and knowledge-sharing is important, it does seem that insufficient attention is being paid to how learners, whether pupils or teachers, use and build knowledge.

So let us follow the advice of Kozulin (1996) and return to the beginning. This chapter opened with four questions. What kinds of learners are we likely to need? What kinds of pedagogical practices are likely to support their learning? What kinds of teachers do we think will be able to offer such support? Where are these teachers and how are they to be supported? The first two questions have been tackled in the previous section. There, a version of developing expertise, to be found both in pupils and in teachers, was suggested. It is echoed by Engeström and Middleton (1996: 4) in their description of expertise as 'ongoing collaborative, and discursive construction of tasks, solutions, visions, breakdowns and innovations' and by Sternberg and Horvath's explanation of expert teachers as people who seek 'to complicate the picture, continually working on the leading edge of their own knowledge and skill' (Sternberg and Horvath, 1995: 13). Learners, it seems, gain most from being with teachers who are alert to the possibilities for action in an experience and to how learners are likely to interpret them.

The focus now turns to the last two questions and particularly to how teachers are helped to become practitioners who are able to help learners recognize, use and transform the knowledge that is available to them. This view of teaching emphasizes the complexity of classrooms as sites for knowledge-generation as well as places where learners are inducted into current understandings. A criticism of sociocultural pedagogy in the previous section signalled that the influence of cognitive anthropology on sociocultural psychology could suggest a pedagogy oriented solely towards induction of learners into existing cultures. But we are suggesting the need for a future-oriented pedagogy. That is, that teaching and teacher education need to adapt to, and critique, the shifting demands of late capitalism and enable learners to become informed participants in democratic communities. Consequently we need to look not only at the practices of teachers as agents in the niches that comprise schooling but also at the affordances for being, seeing and responding, i.e. the practice of teaching, that are to be found within these niches. A sociocultural pedagogy needs to be complemented by an analysis of local affordances at the social level of the niche to examine how affordances for action for theorizing teachers might be enriched.

An analysis at the level of the niche is entirely compatible with a sociocultural approach. Wertsch, for example, explains: 'The goal of the sociocultural approach is to explicate the relationships between human action on the one hand, and the cultural, institutional, and historical situations in which this action occurs, on the other' (Wertsch *et al.*, 1995: 11). This description certainly implies that practices are embedded in cultures and that these cultures provide those varied opportunities for action described by Axel as the 'action potence' in a situation (Axel, 1997). But the relationship between culture and action is complex. Cole discusses context as a weaving together of the elements that constitute and allow the action (Cole, 1996). This weaving together makes distinctions between cognition, action and culture problematic and signals that attention to action requires attention to intention and to affordances. Concepts from cognitive anthropology can be helpful here. Strauss and Quinn, for example, describe culture as 'a fuzzy concept' (Strauss and Quinn, 1997: 7). They discuss cultural construing as part of the process of sharing schema with others while sharing an experience. Consequently they suggest that culture is both within and outside individuals, both shaping and being shaped by them as they interact in and with cultures that are mediated by the resources within them. Mind is being socially formed in the Vygotskian sense, but it is also interacting with and impacting on the cultural niche in which activity is occurring. Cole's notion of weaving, together with an understanding of the fuzzy nature of boundaries between person and culture, points us towards intervention to support the development of practice at the level of the social practices of the niche. When this idea is taken into teacher training we are arguing that training in schools needs be based on more than a good relationship between mentors and student teachers. Instead initial training needs to be incorporated into the pedagogic goals of schools if it is to support student teachers as learners who are to become theorizing teachers.

However, the picture of initial teacher training in England that is emerging in this chapter suggests that the professional minds of student teachers are being shaped to ensure that they are conscientious deliverers of the curriculum. It has also been implied that training partnerships between schools and universities collude in this mind-forming process by relying on agreed planning proforma as the major point of articulation between a student teacher's experiences in the university and in the school. Use of these proforma ensures that student teachers receive the curricular experiences while in school that training programmes are obliged to provide if they are to remain 'compliant' with government requirements. We perhaps need to understand more clearly how these practices have emerged before we can make suggestions about how they might change.

One analysis draws on the version of activity theory currently being developed by Engeström under the broad framework of developmental work research (Engeström et al., 1999). Activity theory, like socio-cultural psychology, is a development from the work of Vygotsky, where Vygotsky's concern with a focus on intentional action is located firmly within a system of social relations. These social relations may be evident in interpersonal interactions and in interactions with objects that have been given cultural meaning within the system. The starting point for enquiry is the system and the interactions within it. In brief, the analytic model offered by Engeström connects (1) an analysis of how actions are mediated by cultural tools to produce outcomes that are culturally acceptable with (2) a framework for understanding how actions and tools have been shaped by the socio-cultural-historical forces within and outside the system in which the action occurs. Importantly, this framework helps us to see that not only are affordances for action differentially distributed across apparently similar activity systems (e.g. classrooms, elementary schools or subject departments), they may be differentially interpreted by individual participants in those systems. An analysis of the interplay of these forces provides a starting point for systemic change undertaken by participants. His analytic model is usually explained in the following way starting at Figure 4 (see Engeström http://www.edu.helsinki.fi/activity).

Figure 4 shows a process of mediated action where the *actor* (or actors), for example a mentor, interacts with the learner (in Engeström's terminology the *object*) in order to produce a specific *learning outcome*. The priority for most schools is, of course, pupil learning outcomes, to which the learning of student teachers comes a clear second. The interaction between mentors and student teachers is mediated by various *cultural tools* (e.g. an artefact, form of behaviour, language use). The argument presented in this chapter suggests that, in England at least, the lesson plan which contains within it the curricular intentions of the university for the student teacher and those of the school for the pupils is likely to be the most important tool. So far, we have been discussing an easily recognizable model of mediated learning. However, to Figure 4 Engeström adds a cultural underpinning, shown in Figure 5 which allows us to see how the mediation process is shaped by, for

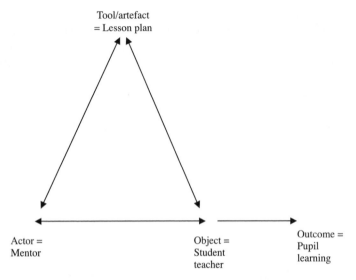

Figure 4 The mediated learning of student teachers using lesson plans

example, the historical expectations of the community in which the action is occurring.

To continue the mentoring illustration, evidence gathered in a school where school-based training is taking place can produce the following picture (Edwards and Ogden, 1999b). The mentors' practices of leaving the student teacher to work in isolation and to focus support on observation and formal feedback can be explained by what the community of the school believes to be in accord with the *rules* of mentoring. The rules governing mentors' practices, as interpreted by the school as a *community*, are a relic of pre-reform arrangements when university tutors did indeed restrict their role to observation and formal feedback. The school as a community has priorities which, in a period of high accountability, centre on pupil performance. Community priorities therefore emphasize effective curriculum coverage and pupil learning outcomes and therefore support student teachers' rigid use of planning proforma. The *division of labour* between colleagues in a school in the support available for student teachers tends to locate responsibility with each mentor. Indeed student teachers and their mentors frequently seem desert-islanded in the midst of school life, connected to that life primarily by involvement in the processes of planning for curriculum coverage. Meanwhile division of labour in the classroom between

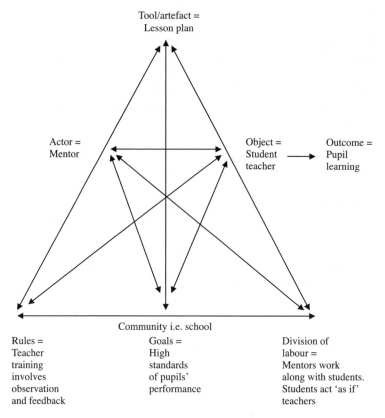

Figure 5 A systemic analysis of mentoring in a school using activity theory

mentors and student teachers indicates that the learners in the class-rooms are the pupils and not the student teachers. Consequently student teachers present themselves as competent performers able to deliver, even when they are in need of periods of what Lave and Wenger (1991) describe as peripheral participation, i.e. learning to interpret classrooms alongside more expert practitioners (Edwards, 1997a). Each of these positions is interconnected and positions mentors as teachers of their pupils by proxy with their intentional action focused on pupils as learners.

This analysis is not an indictment of mentors and schools; instead it offers an opportunity to identify the tensions and contradictions in the system as a starting point for what Engeström terms *expansive learning*, or learning at the systems level. A capacity for learning at the systems level would seem to be essential for organizations adapting to the vicissitudes of postmodernity. The learning that might occur from the analysis just outlined could include a rethinking of the position of student teachers as learners, how mentors might support student teachers by working with pupils alongside them and by offering support for student teachers' learning as a community endeavour.

But each school or training partnership would need to work out its own way of operating, ever mindful of the opportunities for learning available in each socio-cultural-historical context and how they might be differentially interpreted. A relatively novel feature of the model is the opportunity it provides for reading the system historically, making possible insights into how current options for action have been constructed over time. Also as Cole observes, a valuable element of Engeström's analysis is that it doesn't 'privilege production over social cohesion' (Cole, 1995: 140). That is, it does not seek slick solutions in favour of those considered best for the community by the community, on the basis of the evidence produced for the analysis. In addition it allows us to recognize that changes at the systems level make possible changes in the action potence of system and the opportunities for changes in the ways that individuals participate in the system, and therefore for their professional learning.

Communities for learning

Clearly the analytic process just outlined is not offered as a solution and, even as a process for getting some purchase on intentions, behaviours and outcomes, it is provisional. What it offers is a slight shift in attention from an obsession with outcome, which calls for a simplistic focus on cause and effect, to attention to how people learn to think, act and change their environments. That readjusted focus permits an exploration of how people develop the wherewithal to deal with new knowledge, whether that knowledge is simply new to them or is a new development in the community of practice in which they are participating.

Engeström's focus on process, and on the evidence gathered in the system which supports that process, mirrors to an extent that of Scardamalia and Bereiter in their work with pupils on Computer Supported Intentional Learning Environments (CSILE) at the University of Toronto alluded to briefly earlier in this chapter. Scardamalia and Bereiter advocate the development of schools as knowledge-building communities (Scardamalia and Bereiter, 1999). The outcomes of these communities are not necessarily the tangible products so frequently offered as proof of work completed, such as a report or a web page. Instead they include the contributions made to developing understanding within a group of pupils, new understandings that are shared, a capacity for effective problem-solving and reflective revision of previously held ideas. In such a community, the agentic action of both teachers and learners is directed primarily towards a better understanding as an outcome.

The CSILE study finds support from those studies from within a situated cognition tradition which attend to how knowledge is constructed, distributed and used within communities. Bruner, for example, uses the illustration of the successful laboratory in which a shared 'extended intelligence' and ways of thinking and using knowledge are appropriated by new members while participating in its activities (Bruner, 1996b: 154). With a more overt focus on knowledge construction, Gardner discusses the idea of 'expanded intelligence' which he locates in the interactions between individuals (Hatch and Gardner, 1993: 184). Here the suggestion is that the interactions of differently informed participants scaffold mutual understandings.

Importantly, sense-making in each of these examples involve developing understandings in interactions centred on activities, even if these activities are abstract problem-solving tasks such as designing a research study in a laboratory. Knowledge is shared while it is in use while new ways of seeing are constructed in the interaction. Here we see an important shift in emphasis from Piagetian notions (as translated into educational simplifications) of learning by doing, to a focus on learning by using. Here the tools and artefacts of the culture are being used and ways of being, seeing and responding being shaped and developed within the community. An obvious step would seem to be to transfer Bruner's laboratory example to schools so that schools can operate as learning organizations where the products are often simply better understandings.

There is nothing new in the idea of schools as learning communities. But despite decades of effort from both the school improvement or development movement (e.g. Gray et al., 1996) and action researchers (e.g. Elliott, 1991) the practice of teaching in classrooms has changed little. Yet it seems that societal and technological changes will eventually make pedagogical developments imperative. Clearly the profession, if it is to maintain the freedom we have argued to be necessary for a responsive pedagogy, needs to be able to accommodate new demands in systems where the action potence is sufficiently strong and professional agency can be exercised. Learning communities as we have described them do not call for selfish agency but for a relational version of self connected to the common good (Taylor, 1991), engaged in a process of discursive rationality (Benhabib, 1992), supported by a psychology of action which is oriented to ethical questions of being and intention (Shotter, 1993). It is also an agency compelled to seek complexity in pedagogical acts and to develop and share worthwhile responses to interpretations. It is an agency made possible by schools as activity systems, which welcome regular opportunities for rethinking common organizational purposes.

So where is educational research in this vision? In brief, it could be present as forms of teacher research through which teachers increasingly share school data, including observations of practice, to inform their general interpretations and decisions about school purpose. It may also be found in universities, perhaps in multidisciplinary teams such as the authors of this book, which can explore relationships between policy, institutional affordances, learning interactions and individual learning. It may also be found in research partnerships or networks which operate between schools and universities. Just as pupils and teachers have been positioned in this chapter as participants in specific communities who are struggling to interpret features of those communities in increasingly informed ways, educational researchers may be encouraged to develop dispositions to engage with pedagogical research at the point of practice. One outcome of such close-to-practice research would be that university researchers would be able to explore, discursively with teacher colleagues, the affordances for both research and pedagogical action they each can see. Another would be that the theorizing teacher we have argued for would be supported by the wider set of cognitions distributed across the network or partnership.

We already have examples of this kind of work in classrooms, led by researchers who to a greater or lesser degree are working within sociocultural and situated cognition traditions. They include the CSILE project already discussed, the design experiments of A. L. Brown and her colleagues in Oakland, California (Brown, 1992); Wells and Chang-Wells's action-research based work on knowledge-building, again in Toronto (Wells, 1999; Wells and Chang-Wells, 1992). These projects, as sites where the communities of practice of researchers and teachers overlap, may disturb the social practices of schools and universities. They are likely to offer fresh ways of interpreting events, enrich the scientific concepts used in teaching, raise questions about pedagogy and knowledge production and call for reconfigured relationships between the partners and knowledge.

Chaiklin, writing with a Vygotskian perspective on the relationship between theory and practice outlined in our discussion of scientific concepts in Chapter 5, suggests that we need to think of *theory/practice* as an iteration, a to-ing and fro-ing, between what is commonly seen as basic and applied research (Chaiklin, 1993). Theory/practice, in Chaiklin's terms, can both illuminate practice and be incorporated into practices. Close-to-practice research, which keeps its roots in robust theoretical frames, can throw light on immediate pedagogical affordances, can highlight tensions and contradictions at the system level and can become integrated as informed problem-solving into professional practice. Additionally it can itself be open to questions from practice that can help disrupt the assumptions that support theory (see Figure 3, p. 45). Importantly it can ensure that practice remains provisional and is shaped by theorizing teachers – since, like the psychology Shotter advocates (Shotter, 1993: 148, 149), it 'respects the being' of people.

University-based teacher educators who are also researchers are uniquely situated, as social scientists and subject specialists, at points of interconnection between these disciplines and educational practice. Unlike colleagues elsewhere in universities, they are well placed to become engaged researchers aiming at the rethinking practice. In doing so, they can make their contribution to initial training by supporting schools as learning communities and fit places for the professional development of beginning teachers. And they can enrich the continuing professional development of teachers by supporting and informing teachers' engagement with knowledge as users and producers of knowledge of teaching. Suggestions for rethinking school–university relationships are not new (Edwards 1997b; Edwards and Collison, 1996; Firestone and Pennell, 1997; Huberman, 1995). However, a shift of focus away from research as simply knowledge accumulation, and professional development as primarily the application of that knowledge, may assist the rethinking of those social practices and the relationships within them that might support the development of informed, responsive, theorizing teachers.

Chapter 7

Rethinking teacher education

In this chapter we attempt to bring together the strands of what a new teacher education might look like. We begin with a brief restatement of the argument in Chapter 6. We go on to suggest why, now, this will resonate at one and the same time with contemporary culture *and* with an emergent neo-Fordist work regime within an increasingly service-sector economy. Whilst the disciplinary purists and quick-fix, certainty-seeking politicians may have little truck with our conclusion – that is to say, we do not seek to proselytize *a big-t Truth* for teacher education – we suggest that teaching, in a culturally and intellectually complex society, cannot be reduced to neat solutions which the tidy-minded can live with. We end with the implications of our arguments for teacher professionalism.

In the last five chapters we have attempted to work with the three themes outlined in Chapter 1 in order to challenge the simple certainties which are offered as responses to the ambivalences and uncertainties within which teacher educators are trying to do their best for learners in schools. In pursuing these themes we have attempted to begin to meet the challenges and limits to teacher education produced by late capitalism, through analyses of the conditions it has created for teacher education and through critical consideration of the conceptual tools with which educators can rethink teaching and therefore teacher education.

In the previous chapter we argued that managing the shifting orientations of learners to knowledge was one of the major challenges facing the teaching profession in the present phase of late capitalism. By also looking at teachers' learning as a continuous reorientation to knowledge, we proposed that those responsible for education policies and practices should not limit educational enquiry to gathering evidence of what has worked so that it can be given to practitioners as a blueprint for pedagogy. Instead, teacher education should embrace the opportunities for professional development found in a view of expertise as a capacity to interpret and respond to the complexities of practice in increasingly informed ways. We were therefore arguing for teaching as informed interpretation and deliberative action. Teachers' responsible actions, we suggested, will be enhanced if teachers are seen as users and producers of knowledge about teaching, in communities of practice which are constantly refreshed through processes of professional inquiry, in partnerships between practitioners and researchers. We were therefore drawing on understandings of communities of learners which emphasize the extended intelligence of the community.

We characterized teacher professionalism as a version of self-authoring and responsible deliberation, where decision-making was influenced by the affordances of local contexts (i.e. by what is permissible in a context) and by teachers' capacities to interpret and use those affordances. We were not arguing for a relativist version of education where different communities offer different life opportunities to pupils. However, we were implying that schools could benefit from analysing themselves as cultural systems with specific histories, which shape both local affordances and the ways they are interpreted. Such analyses have the potential to reveal local opportunities for pupils and teachers to be users and producers of knowledge, and to inform the design of school-level responses which enable teachers and learners to participate in the knowledge economies of late capitalism. To an extent this is also what we are attempting to achieve with teacher education in our book.

Even if one accepts a functionalist association between education and the economy we still do not believe that an overly prescriptive and bureaucratic approach to pedagogy on the part of the government is functional for the new economy; and nor will it resonate with the complexities of contemporary culture. In sum, the reasons for this are as follows. For the past two hundred years, the pedagogical style in our schools has altered little. In an age of mass-production, overseen by Fordist management principles, the traditional whole-class didactic teaching style had much to commend it in terms of its relevance to the world of work. The architecture of schools varied little. Pupils were preferred quite literally in uniform. It was efficient and formal. But let us turn to some prominent commentators on the new economy. They argue that workers are becoming disenchanted with the impersonalities of rational management styles.

In her *Charismatic Capitalism: Direct Selling Organizations in America*, Biggart (1989) concludes: 'Firms, I believe, have begun to reach the limits of rationality as a strategy for controlling workers [. . .] Independent work that relies on solidarity, respect, or mutual trust, is poorly served by bureaucratic structures that create authority differences' (pp. 169–70). (It is perhaps telling that the issue of trust in organizations is now a topical issue: see, for example, the special issue on 'Trust In and Between Organizations' in the *Academy of Management Review*, 1998.) The workplace is now seen not just as a bureaucratic structure but as a lived culture, a shared and socially constructed site in which one's identity can be recognized and rewarded. Bauman (1998) has argued that now, in this consumerist culture, workers apply aesthetic criteria to their work, the value of which 'is judged by its capacity to generate pleasurable experience' (p. 32). If we substitute the term 'schools' for 'jobs' in the following extract, then it is possible to see how important it is that the pedagogy for the new economy of late capitalism accords with the expectations which consumer culture now affords (most) young people:

> Like everything else which may reasonably hope to become the target of desire and an object of free consumer choice, jobs must be 'interesting' – varied, exciting, allowing for adventure, containing certain (though not excessive) measures of risk, and giving occasion to ever-new sensations. Jobs that are monotonous, repetitive, routine, unadventurous, allowing no initiative and promising no challenge to wits nor a chance for self-testing and self-assertion, are 'boring'.
>
> (p. 38)

Those jobs (and schools) which do not pass this 'aesthetic test' will be filled (or tolerated) only by those faced by necessity rather than desire.

What kind of worker does this new economy need? In *End of Millennium*, the third volume of his three-volume work *The Information Age: Economy, Society and Culture*, Castells distinguishes between two kinds of labour: generic and self-programmable. Generic workers are the classic 'hands' of the nineteenth-century factory floor. They are assigned tasks and they execute them:

> These 'human terminals' can, of course, be replaced by machines, or by any other body around the city, the country or the world,

depending on business decisions. While they are collectively indispensable to the production process, they are individually expendable.

(Castells, 1997b: 340)

In Castells's terminology, generic workers are 'warehoused' as opposed to 'educated'. But not so the self-programmable worker: for this worker has the 'capacity constantly to redefine the necessary skills for a given task, and to access the sources for learning these skills. Whoever is educated, in the proper organizational environment, can reprogram him/herself toward the endlessly changing tasks of the production process' (p. 340). Those who are unemployable form the 'legions of discarded, devalued people [who] form the growing planet of the irrelevant' (Castells, 2000: 12). In sum, 'I think, therefore I produce' (Castells, 1997b: 359).

This brings us to our point that this new economy – if it is to be a knowledge-based economy comprising a high proportion of self-programmable workers – requires a new pedagogy of the type proposed in the previous chapter. Within the workplace, it will not suffice to reassert what Clegg (1999) calls exploitative learning which is 'focused on making tasks explicit and task cycles short and routine [. . .] In this model learning is best accomplished through explicitness about rules – the core of much organization theory since F.W. Taylor' (p. 261). What is needed is exploratory learning which 'is associated with complex search, basic research, innovation, variation, risk – taking a more relaxed control' (p. 262). If teachers are treated as if they are Castells's generic workers, then it is unlikely that they will be able to produce self-programmable school-leavers. If teachers are seen as competing individuals in the pursuit of performance-related pay, then their collegiality will be reduced. We are saying that cognition does not reside solely in the individual pupil, but collectively, a distributed sociocultural production. Equally, we are saying that professionalism is itself a sociocultural production which is not contained within the confines of the classroom but which includes broader networks beyond it. Teacher professionalism and pupils' learning are both networked, socially distributed processes. Which is not to say that they should be given free rein. These communities have constraints placed upon them – official and otherwise – but within these boundaries the means of production, so to say, will be a collaborative one. Nor is it to say that what counts as knowledge about how to teach and learn is the outcome of a consensus which is only locally arrived at, for these local constructions interact with those academic communities whose endeavours are more to do with the production of public and formal theory. In sum, whilst highly dirigiste control by governments over teachers will probably be cheaper and efficient in the near term (though the high costs of surveillance could offset this), it is unlikely that it will be effective for the new economy. Standardization and efficiency-savings may turn out to be a false economy.

So much for the economy. What of society? It bears reminding ourselves that we are witnessing not only the emergence of a flexible and highly productive economy but also a society which is unstable and which gives rise to great anxieties. But, whilst the economy is being liberalized, the society must somehow coalesce socially. Here lies the difficulty:

> As much as we need to liberalize the economy we must 'solidarize' or unify the society. But this cannot be done by invoking the traditional family or taking refuge in fundamentalist values . . . Since the individual can no longer return to the lost paradise of a structured stable world (the job, the family, the community, the union, the church, the state) she/he will have to learn to patch life together with a set of half-certainties.
>
> (Carnoy and Castells, 1997: 53)

A contemporary pedagogy must prepare the young for society as well as for the economy. This society is risky. Anxiety needs to be coped with. Castells (2000: 21) suggests that it can be coped with in two typical ways: 'on the one hand, self-reliant communes, anchored in their non-negotiable sets of beliefs; and on the other hand, networks of ever shifting individuals'. Arrangements for learning and teaching in the school which enable networks (or communities) to be formed and reformed will serve both economy and society better than those which continue to reassert a dated back-to-basics philosophy.

The implications of our arguments for teacher education are considerable. The simplistic view of knowledge we have identified as objectivist creates a very simple relationship between the teacher and the taught, with the teacher acting as a mere conduit, channelling a fixed knowledge-base to the learner (this pattern of learning being of course duplicated in the teacher–pupil context). Teacher education would then consist of little more than showing student teachers how to pass on that knowledge in the most effective way possible, with questions about how that knowledge has been identified and what is to count as 'effective' being irrelevant. The position could be summarized as being of the form, 'Here the knowledge; there the learner – you, the teacher or teacher educator, now deliver.'

In fact, as we have argued, this is precisely the situation that the English education system finds itself in. In spite of well-documented critiques of both the National Curriculum for schools (Lawton and Chitty, 1998) and the National Curriculum for teacher education (Wilkin, 1999), these two necessarily related curricula provide the flesh that gives life to the form of argument identified above. One strand of our own critique of objectivist arguments about the nature of knowledge has been that the English government's objectivist approach to the National Curricula is not one that can be justified, only enforced through crude political fiat. The implication for teachers', and teacher educators', professionalism is that they have neither autonomy nor for that matter control of what is to count as appropriate knowledge in their chosen field: it is for this reason that we have talked about the audits run by OFSTED as one of policing teachers and teacher educators, ensuring that they do in fact carry out what is required of them by their respective National Curricula.

However, if we were to take the contextualist approach advanced in this book then the curriculum for teacher education would be radically altered. Teacher educators (in England at least) would no longer find themselves having to operate with some form of Sartre's bad-faith (Sartre 1943, chapter 2, *passim*), working as modernists within a post-modern context. Instead, they would be able to work through the implications of operating with conceptions of uncertain knowledge. This would require them to accept arguments we have advanced here drawn from versions of sociology, philosophy and psychology, their thrust being a simple one, namely that:

- economic pressures on teacher education create a centralizing effect on provision, but the social contexts within which teacher education operates produce diversity
- there was once a strong philosophical research agenda aimed at producing a single objectivist account of knowledge, but modern philosophical approaches to knowledge do not support, indeed explicitly reject, such attempts, preferring to locate knowledge-claims within a social, rule-governed, context

- an objectivist and unconditional analysis of learning and teaching based on a flawed view of knowledge is in opposition to a communitarian approach to learning which makes the various practices of teaching inevitably provisional and conditional on the contexts within which they operate and which give them meaning.

These have been presented above as sets of dichotomies. However, we have argued against dichotomous approaches, preferring instead arguments of the type 'both-and' over 'either-or'. The result is that teacher educators are placed in a much more dynamic position than the one many currently find themselves in, as they are operating with both of the positions that represent the dichotomies above. They are enabled to see more clearly the complex, potentially contradictory, contexts within which they operate in ways we have already examined. They are thus able to reassert their autonomy as professionals in order that they might provide similar multiple and flexible approaches to understanding learning from a communitarian perspective.

A working example of this approach would be Farr Darling's in Canada, as reported in her recent paper (2001). She identifies 'community of inquiry' as meaning a 'collective pursuit of knowledge and understanding' (p. 8) and shows how applying such a notion to her pre-service student teachers changed the way the course was experienced. For Farr Darling:

> Ideally, a community of inquiry is purposeful and inclusive, a place for shared knowledge, communication of new ideas, and critical dialogue about those ideas . . . Teacher educators have good reason to believe that if genuine communities of inquiry can be created with all interested parties (teacher educators, school based educators and preservice teachers) the benefits would be significant. This is because the structure and communicative practices of a community of inquiry potentially address criticisms that have been levelled at many existing professional programs: fragmentation between faculties of education and schools, duplication and overlap of course content and assignments, and no time for reflection. A working community of inquiry could bring together the agendas of school and campus by creating space for dialogue and an opportunity to find common intellectual ground . . . Finally, a community of inquiry could consider questions about teaching and learning that would enrich both school experiences and

university classes, and give preservice teachers the tools to reflect on their emerging practices.

(2001: 19)

This is something she has tried with three cohorts of students, and she is under no illusions that there are no difficulties with the approach. However, her argument is that these difficulties are far outweighed by the benefits, to students, teachers and teacher educators.

We pause here to summarize the course which teacher education has taken. Table 3 (p. 80), when read from left to right, reveals an initial sense of intellectually driven certainty in teacher education, a certainty which, in the 1970s and 1980s, is called into question, both by academics and by practitioners. In the 1990s, the 'confusion' is removed, as central government imposes a new certainty. This was the point which we reached in Chapter 4. In Chapters 5 and 6, we set out our alternative: a teacher education whose theoretical basis is sociocultural; whose locus of control is multiple and diffuse – that is, networked; and whose effects will in all likelihood be beneficial for a new economy. But its effects would also enhance democracy, for our alternative could begin to render pedagogy and schooling as more collaborative, more communal and more open to variety, debate and difference.

To elaborate: the themes that we have constructed our book around, in particular the combined impacts of a simplistic policy-driven approach to teacher education, the loss of certainty and its replacement by a paradox of uncertainty, with all the implications these developments have for learning, can be seen as representing way-marks for those attempting to chart the topography of teacher education today. One way of making sense of the confusion that such a complex map produces is to opt for an approach which concentrates simply on the structures which define teacher education, and this is precisely what the English government has attempted. The apparent success of this approach brings with it a considerable cost to those at the cutting edge of education – teacher educators, teachers and pupils – in that they find themselves forced into a simplistic structure which does not map on to the complex world they actually experience.

Our contention is that rethinking structures is not an appropriate way of representing and addressing the complexities of teacher education in post-Fordist cultures. Instead the professionalism of teachers, based upon a more subtle understanding of the relationships that exist between knowledge, society, schools and learners, is what requires rethinking. We suggest that a way forward is the contextualist approach to teacher education argued for here, where teachers and teacher educators inform and contest the core knowledge that underpins their actions as professionals.

We are not proposing an easy option when we argue for a teacher education which creates theorizing teachers who use and develop what Vygotsky described as scientific concepts, as opposed to everyday concepts, about pedagogy (see Chapter 5) while they support learners. The insertion of the term 'scientific concept' into the language game that is teacher education is to assert the hermeneutic version of science that Charles Taylor has argued is best suited to developing learning theory (Taylor, 1985: 130). The scientific concepts that are used by theorizing and interpreting teachers are, as Vygotsky explained in general terms (Vygotsky, 1987), rooted in the world as it is experienced. But they also allow practitioners to disembed analyses and inform the more extensive understandings held within the professional community and so illuminate the interpretations and meaning making of others. However, a Vygotskian take on scientific concepts adds a further fundamental feature to distinguish what we are describing as contextulist from objectivist models of knowledge and its use. In his description of scientific concepts and their relation to the world, Vygotsky carefully pointed out that we use existing concepts to interrogate the world. Therefore we need to be open to examining the ways in which we interrogate the facts that are apparent to us. His comments, written in the mid-1920s, still resonate when we argue that theorizing teachers can illuminate their practices through engagement with self-critical social sciences, which are themselves developed as a result of contact with the world of practice:

> does not the very selection of the concepts needed to know these facts require an analysis of the concepts in addition to the analysis of the facts? After all, if concepts as tools, were set aside for particular facts of experience in advance, all science would be superfluous: then a thousand administrators-regulators or statistician-counters could note down the universe on cards, graphs and columns. Scientific knowledge differs from the registration of a fact in that it selects the concept needed, i.e. it analyses both fact and concept.
>
> (Vygotsky, 1987: 251)

The professionalism and professional learning we are proposing repositions teachers. Currently teachers and teacher educators, particularly in

England (but the tendency is evident elsewhere) are required to deliver the curriculum as sets of segmented tasks to pupils and to reflect on their own practices in order to enhance the efficiency of their delivery. We are suggesting that they engage at a conceptual level not only with the knowledge-base that underpins their deliberative action but also with the ways in which that knowledge-base is constructed, contested and developed. This degree of control over a professional knowledge-base would seem to be a prerequisite for any claims to be professional. But perhaps more importantly it would seem to be a prerequisite for a knowledge-base that is rooted not simply in what has worked in the past but in informed interpretations of current contexts in all their complexity. Clearly we are not simply rethinking the initial preparation of teachers here. None the less, developing a capacity for interrogating assumptions, both local and general, should arguably be a basic intention for a programme aiming at helping student teachers to become theorizing and interpreting professionals who are able to work intelligently with others when meeting new demands and opportunities – and ultimately to interrogate and inform how we construct, contextualise and develop the core knowledge of pedagogy.

Control of the core is central to control of the profession. Evidence and its trustworthiness are currently invoked to maintain government control of the core. Evidence-based or evidence-informed practice is currently promoted by government agencies in England as an underpinning of the new professionalism. The concept is used in at least two language-games in education policy-making. The first game is clearly objectivist and in its own terms rigorous. There, policy-valued knowledge about teaching is checked by researchers using randomized control trials and subsequently offered to professionals as 'what works'. The second game, when set up to support the implementation of policy, is slightly more complex and at first sight appears contextualist. It employs the language of professional empowerment through researching practice. It may even involve removing teachers from the constraining contexts of their own schools to create new professional identities through participating in teacher research networks. Local knowledge is constructed in these networks through the examination of practice and the implementation of new strategies which are shared with other teachers using language that is easily understood. The trustworthiness here lies in the face validity of the research tales that teachers tell each other. The use of scientific constructs is discouraged as they impede clarity. So regulated is the curriculum, however, that the new strategies described are aimed at more effective curriculum delivery rather than at, for example, rethinking how pupils relate to knowledge as producers as well as users (in passing it is worth noting that those who police the tightly regulated curriculum appear to behave like Vygotsky's 'thousand administrators', noting down teachers' 'universe' on their OFSTED cards). Higher education participation in the second game creates a tension unless the university researcher goes with the grain of policy certainty. Consequently the protective belt of assumptions around the policy-driven and objectivist core beliefs about teaching remains undisturbed.

A rather different notion of evidence-based practice is implied by our picture of the theorizing teacher who uses conceptual tools both to question certainty and to produce responses to uncertainty which are anchored in a consideration of the relationships that exist between knowledge, society, schools and learners. Theorizing teachers focus on the principles on which theory can be built as much as on the answers that theory can produce. Once again we can turn to Vygotsky for advice for the tentatively risk-taking and theorizing teacher. Talking of the need for tentativeness in sense-making, he described the process as 'limping towards the truth' (Vygotsky, 1987: 266). When they examine the processes of sense-making, theorizing teachers can note how knowledge, including the knowledge checked in randomized control trials, is used, transformed, generated and shared in learning communities and they can question simple certainties without sliding into relativism.

Teaching as the social control of children executing tasks as they are warehoused through the education system is already proving to be an unattractive profession and not only in England (Cockburn, 2000; Macdonald, 1999). Resistance to teaching as a profession is in part because the exercise of deliberative agency is currently particularly restricted (Edwards, 2001). But it is also because the education system reflects the *zeitgeist* of the nineteenth century. We have no option but to rethink teaching and teacher education in order to capture the possibilities to be found in the present learning *zeitgeist*. To do so would give teachers access to the excitement that new understandings of pedagogy bring.

We are therefore, tentatively at least, arguing for more teacher education; for a teacher education which is informed by close-to-practice versions of the social sciences, among which we would include history; for a teacher education which is not limited to curriculum and how it is delivered; and for a teacher education geared towards creating teachers who seek and interrogate uncertainty.

Chapter 8

Delivering deliverance

David Hamilton
(Institutionen för Pedagogik, Umeå University, Sweden)

'We wondered', wrote one of the authors in January 2001, 'if you could do your 3,000 to 4,000 words before the end of March?' Such was the concise invitation to react to the earlier chapters of this manuscript. The hope was that I might respond with some historical reflections.

The task has not been easy. But it has been instructive. I had not participated in the earlier discussions that surrounded the creation of the earlier chapters; nor did I know their origins or history. I am not writing an article from scratch; I am not writing a preface, an *hors d'oeuvres* to the text; nor am I writing a review of a separate work, something that will appear at a different time, and in a different place.

Overall, it has been difficult to find an image to steer my writing. I am not composing an oration, obituary, salutation or farewell. At best, I feel a late but honoured participant in a conversation about teaching and learning.

It has not been easy to join the conversation. The authors have adopted a very broad canvas. Their ideas are expressed in many colours and shades; and they had left many parts of their oeuvre in the form of incomplete but suggestive outlines. Nor is their text propositional. It does not culminate in a manifesto. It is incorrigibly open and discursive. What, for instance, should I make of the following sentence: 'One feature that appears to be common to many of these government-driven changes is the lack of any substantial rational support for them *other than perhaps the rationale of the market*' (Chapter 1, p. 3, emphasis added). What is the significance of the emphasized subsidiary clause? And how does 'perhaps' modulate the meaning? If the sentence is reduced to a single proposition, should it be 'government-driven changes lack rational support'? Or 'government-driven changes are supported by the rationale of the market'?

In fact, to understand the double reference to the market, it is necessary to read the entire text. At second or third reading, I can appreciate the authors' circumlocution. The form of the sentence is a comment on contrary rationalities, or regimes of truth. Different rationalities are inscribed in educational thought and practice. The relegation of the logic of the marketplace to a sub-clause indicates that the writers do not rate it as highly as other rationalities. In other words, the authors do not believe that education is a private 'good' that can be commodified, branded and, in turn, bought and sold as a commodity.

This position on the political structuring of education becomes clear as their argument unfolds. But it is not the primary focus of their attention. Instead, they give more attention to a different golden thread – the recurrent tension between performativity and democracy in the work of teachers and teacher educators.

Performativity relates to the performance of teaching, itself the outcome of teacher education. Moreover, attention to performativity challenges the theoreticism of the academy, including the institutions of teacher education. It focuses on something else; that is, how teachers act in the schoolroom. Thus *Rethinking Teacher Education* engages with the manifestations and consequences of performativity – everything from performance-related pay, through reflective practice, to action research. And it also engages with judging such practices against current versions of the Enlightenment project – the emancipation of all humankind. In short, the contents of *Rethinking Teacher Education* grapple with a recurrent tension in the political order, the reconciliation of individual rights with the collective 'good'.

The authors' argument has three elements. First, the organisation and conduct of teacher education has, on an international scale, been reduced to simple certainties. Second, these certainties do not correspond to the lifeworld of teachers or teacher trainers; and, third, this deep tension can be challenged through a variety of 'antidotes', one of which (in my terms) is the analysis of performativity and democracy in education.

In advancing these themes, the text sets off hares which scatter in all directions. I found this diaspora of ideas engaging, and provocative. I often felt that every paragraph invited line-by-line reaction. But it would be cavalier, not to say draining and counterproductive, to follow such a strategy in this review. Other readers can take up that challenge. Here, instead, I keep my comments close to the three terms that, I believe, animate the argument of *Rethinking Teacher Education*.

In each case, too, my comments also pay attention to the historical record.

Rule-following and the norm

Rethinking Teacher Education cites the *Communist Manifesto* (1847), saying that 'all that is solid melts into air'. The authors extend this claim about fluidity to the present day – in its commentary on 'locally relevant knowledge' (Chapter 5, p. 100), 'risk-taking' (Chapter 8, p. 134), 'limited certainties' (Chapter 3, p. 51) and 'personally arrived at pedagogies' (Chapter 6, p. 85). These, they suggest, are the certainties that they celebrate. Indeed, as the Hegelian Karl Marx might have also added, change and uncertainty are the only constants. Elsewhere, Marx also noted that to define is also to negate – in the sense that definitions freeze the enduring feature of language-use, its dynamism and creativity.

This problem of frozen language is deeply embedded in the history of teacher education. Terms stay the same, even if their meanings are constantly changing. The term 'normal' school provides an example. The standard explanation, which I inherited, is that 'normal' comes from the Latin word for a rule: *norma*. Thus, students who attended the Glasgow Normal School in the 1830s were learning the rules of teaching. Indeed, this is what I have always taught. And, for precedents, I have always been able to draw attention to the *Écoles Normales* that still exist in France.

But I have recently come to question this explanation. In a recent collection on the history of statistics (Stigler, 2000), there is an essay, by Stigler and Kruskal, on 'Normative terminology'. Much of the essay, of course, relates to the use of 'norm' in statistics (e.g. the normal curve); but it also extends the discussion to normal schools. The authors report that the earliest known use of 'normal school' was not *l'École Normale* established in Paris in 1794 but, rather, a school created in Vienna in the 1760s. Further, the existence of this Austrian *normalschule* also challenges the standard explanation of norm. It was not a teacher training institution but, instead, 'an exemplary school for *children*, a school exhibiting stringent educational norms as a model'. Nevertheless, this Viennese school also had an ancillary purpose 'as a training facility for teachers'. The new name was 'wildly successful', suggest Stigler and Kruskal: 'the connotations of the word "normal" were so attractive and powerful that the teachers in effect took it away from the children and appropriated it for adults' (pp. 426–7).

Stigler and Kruskal's analysis aroused my curiosity, for at least two reasons. First, their analysis includes the word 'model' rather than 'rule', and, second, I do not find their evidence persuasive about the subsequent appropriation of the term 'normal' for other educational institutions. In search of elucidation, I turned to the standard Latin dictionary (Lewis and Short, 1969). *Norma* is defined as rule, but also appears as 'pattern' or 'precept'. Further, one of the sources for *norma* given by Lewis and Short comes from Cicero: *vitam ad certam rationis normam dirigere* (to direct life towards a definite/certain/sure model of procedure).

The Cicero citation caught my attention. Although a classical author, Cicero was also a major figure in the reform of education in the Renaissance and Reformation. In both contexts, education specifically entailed re-forming (cf. reshaping) learners in accordance with classical ideals – of the kind expressed in the writings of Cicero, Quintilian and others. This strand of humanist thought is sometimes known as neo-Platonism, because Plato made recurrent reference to education as the realization of an ideal. Thus, schooling can be built upon idealizations of the learner or the teacher, without necessarily being based on rules. Children can be raised according to ideals, just as teachers can be trained according to ideals.

This alternative explanation of normal schooling is only a hypothesis. But it would explain the fact that, in its early meaning, a normal school could be designed for students of any age. Nevertheless, norms-as-ideals can be readily reduced to norms-as-rules. But there is a generic problem raised by efforts to freeze language in the form of definitions or certainties. It ignores the fact that practice includes not merely an object but also a set of processes that create (or re-form) that object. Further, both object and process can be normative. My teaching is based on a model of the good learner *and* on a model of what I regard as good teaching. Further, I also know that this distinction between normal (or normative) means and normal ends was also a feature of classical philosophy (see Burnet, 1905: 2–3).

Unreachable goals

The tension between norms as rules and norms as ideals has, therefore, an analogy in another feature of performativity – the relation between rules and goals. Celestial navigation provides an example. For many years mariners steered by the stars. They never reached the stars but, nevertheless, achieved their goals. Thus it is possible, in education as well as in seafaring, to distinguish goals to reach and goals to steer by. The writings of Cicero, Plato and many contemporary educationists give more attention to the latter.

Rule-following has another noteworthy feature. Performativity entails a Cartesian view of teaching. It assumes that rule-following will eventually lead to the desired outcomes. Indeed, this was a fundamental assumption in Descartes's *Discourse on Method* (1637):

> These long chains of reasoning had given me cause to imagine that everything is linked in the same way, and that, provided one abstains from accepting any for true [*sic*] which is not true, and that one keeps the right order for one thing to be deduced from that which precedes it, there can be nothing so distant that one does not reach it eventually, or so hidden that one cannot discover it.
>
> (Descartes, 1968: 41, abridged)

Unfortunately, teaching in the twenty-first century is not Cartesian. The initial premises or 'truths' of teaching are not universally accepted. There is always a measure of uncertainty in their formulation and, as a consequence, in the consequences of rule-following. Different premises lead to different processes and different outcomes.

Long ago, Aristotle also recognized that the premises of practice are problematic. For this reason, he distinguished *logic* from *dialectic*. Logical premises are true, while dialectical premises are merely widely accepted. Aristotle was inclined to assume that widely accepted truths *are* true and, therefore, saw logic and dialectic as synonymous. The slippage between the truth status of logic and dialectic was recognized in the sixteenth century (i.e. by the Reformation). Teaching could be seen, therefore, as a true process of logical delivery; or it could be seen as the delivery of inconclusive propositions (quasi-truths). From the latter perspective, what could not be established through logic was made up – bolstered or protected – with the aid of rhetorical devices. Teaching, that is, was a form of argumentation, not the establishment of truths.

Discussions about teaching as a process of argumentation became, therefore, part of the same debates that exercised theology and jurisprudence (legal theory). In effect, teachers delivered lessons in the same sense that preachers delivered sermons and lawyers delivered speeches

– 'for' or 'against' – in the conduct of a trial. In each case, argumentation (dialectic plus rhetoric) was intended to assure assent in the minds of pupils, congregations and juries. Indeed, sixteenth-century dialectics provided the basis for the emergence of didactics in the seventeenth century.

From the perspective of modern (i.e. post-Renaissance) schooling, therefore, educational practice has never been a closed system. It has always entailed the management of uncertainty. Yet it is equally true that some educationists (born-again Cartesians) have repeatedly claimed argumentation as logic and, as a result, educational practice as the following of self-evident certainties.

Another source of uncertainty in educational practice is found outside argumentation – in the vagaries of context. The authors of *Rethinking Teacher Education* suggest that the impact of context is relatively recent. They may be correct. Discussion of context has featured in the philosophy of science only since the beginning of the twentieth century (cf. Einstein's theories of relativity). And it came to prominence only in the latter half of the twentieth century. Within research on teaching, for instance, a classic analysis of the impact of context is Donald Campbell and Julian Stanley's elaboration of 'factors jeopardizing internal and external validity' in their paper on 'Experimental and Quasi-experimental designs for research on teaching (1963: 175ff).

The creation of linear Cartesian rationales was part of the attempt to decontextualize science by re-creating it as a closed system of laboratory experiments and/or mathematical relationships, themselves free from the external threats to validity identified by Campbell and Stanley. Nevertheless, the arguments about uncertainty in *Rethinking Teacher Education* undoubtedly have a contemporary value. They are a welcome antidote to the ideals of performativity, goal-based practice and the audit society (see Power, 1999), as well as the implication of these in the commodification and marketization of education.

Lifeworlds, willpower and world-views

As this heading suggests, power and persuasion have always been part of educational practice. I often feel that education should be envisaged as a little-understood process of enabling people to do things they cannot do; or, to be more charitable, to help people go beyond what they can do. But education can also have a contrary purpose – to help people *not* to do things that they can do. The exertion of power and the ascription of empowerment are not synonymous.

Moreover, I also think it is worth remembering that the limiting case of education practice is not one teacher and one pupil but, rather, self-instruction (i.e. where the teacher and learner are the same person). The lifeworld of education is charged with these social relations and intentions, themselves mediated in a multitude of ways (through curricula, textbooks and other educational media). Moreover, when education (or leading out) is reduced to schooling (or dumbing down), learning and instruction are steered by norms and models that may not be intrinsic to the world-view of those who are the subject of such schooling. School students may be looking for an education whereas, in fact, they are receiving a schooling. The uncertainties that animate education at the start of the twenty-first century, and, more particularly, animated the preparation of *Rethinking Teacher Education*, may arise from the clash of certainties – and practices – entertained by different rationalities or regimes of truth. Every theory entertains certainties; but a plurality of certainties also constitutes a state of uncertainty or, as it is sometimes expressed, incommensurability. Uncertainties arise from a multiplicity of contrary certainties.

I came across a striking example of the impact of contrary certainties as I struggled with this chapter. Standard texts on the history of the Jesuits report that their educational efforts were neither directed to teaching reading (cf. primary education), nor to the professions (e.g. medicine). Yet, it is also the case that the South American city of São Paulo was founded by the Jesuits in 1554 and that the leading Jesuit in this process, Father Anchieta, is celebrated as the author of the first grammar of the coastal indigenous language (Tupi). In effect, the context of Anchieta's missionary responsibilities overshadowed his primary educational task. In distant provinces, Jesuit priests and schoolteachers operated beyond constraints imposed from the centre. They were expected to perform in particular ways; but the context of their missionary work proved to be an overriding 'context'.

The 'uncertainties' identified by the authors of *Rethinking Teacher Education* may have arisen in a similar way. What the authors describe as uncertainty might just as easily be described as interference patterns (of turbulence) created at the intersection of different ways of thinking. Here are three examples of turbulence created by the challenges to certainty. The first comes from the Middle Ages, when European schooling was dominated by the Christian church. At that time, much could be taught from classical sources (e.g. Aristotle, Quintilian and Cicero). In the eyes of the church, however, classical sources were problematic because they were profane (i.e. not Christian).

A long struggle ensued over the status of classical texts. Resolution is commonly attributed to Thomas Aquinas, whose reconciliation of Aristotelian (i.e. classical) logic and Christian revelation provided the church with a powerful intellectual power base. In short, Christians acquired 'reasons to believe' (cf. Audi, 2001: 2).

The second instance of contrary certainties came with the emergence of doctrines that could be propagated by localized community churches (i.e. the forerunners of Protestantism). Local truths came into conflict with truths propagated by the central authorities of the church. Further, the reconciliation of these different certainties was complicated by two social processes: the (mis)translation of doctrines from Latin into vernacular languages (e.g. German); and the use of movable type (pioneered by Gutenberg) to create textbooks with their own assent-seeking structures.

The translators of the Bible, like the designers of textbooks, struggled with an uncertainty built into their practice: delivery does not assure deliverance. Educational agencies may foster delivery (a process), but deliverance (an outcome) is something else. It is often assumed that a Cartesian accumulation of short-term objectives inexorably provides a stairway to the stars. The net result, however, is another version of the Star Wars fantasy: that (1) what can be imagined can be delivered; and (2) that delivery assured deliverance.

Deconstruction of this fantasy is at the heart of *Rethinking Teacher Education*. Practice is never pure. It is always inscribed in – and by – a set of circumstances that, in turn, mediate the intended practice or delivery. In so far as teaching is about the contextualization of intentions and ideals, it is always a political practice. It is about the allocation of resources. Assumptions (reasons to believe) about professional development cannot be accepted as self-evident. They must also be contextualized. If competence development is deemed to be important, do busy persons have the time to engage in it? Do schoolteachers have sufficient resources to realize their own goals as well as the goals allocated by the commonwealth, state or parents? A failure of performance can be a failure of logic, but it can also be a case where context fights back.

Antidotes, not panaceas

To use a term favoured by the authors of *Rethinking Teacher Education*, the question to ask is: are such contextualization practices *affordable* in the political economy of the schoolroom? The political economy of certainty (or delivery) is not the political economy of classroom deliver-ables. Nor is it synonymous with the political economy of a democracy (deliverance). To use another term from *Rethinking Teacher Education*, each is an 'antidote'. It interrupts and problematizes certainties associated with the other.

Teacher education is still deeply implicated in a pedagogic project that, itself, is intimately linked to a democratic, Enlightenment and modernist project of deliverance. In the early days of modern schooling, teaching entailed 'framing' young people (and, sometimes, their parents) to disciplines and identities associated with different social positions and prospects. As such, schooling was an expression of the prevailing power-knowledge relations (or tensions) in society. Education, in the sense of leading out, was a praxis that fostered social mobility (social production) whereas schooling fostered social stasis (or reproduction). In the sixteenth century, these different pro-cesses have been described, by Grafton and Jardine (1986, *passim*), as the difference between teaching humanism, on the one hand, and teaching the humanities, on the other. Humanities were taught to a wide audience (of males) as a means of raising them to take positions (e.g. as diplomats, treasury officials) in the newly emergent state; whereas humanism was taught to young men to assure their inherited social status in later life.

This tension – between education and schooling – found its expres-sion in the educational practices of the eighteenth century. The Enlightenment raised the spectre that all human beings should be given access to the cultural capital associated with liberty, equality and fraternity. In fact, of course, the fruits of these political aspirations only became affordances for the white, male, bourgeoisie. Nevertheless, this contextual consequence – the association of different forms of schooling with differences in social class, gender, race and 'ability' – has been widely contested. And it is a contestation that survives to the present day, and that is deeply inscribed in *Rethinking Teacher Education*.

Conclusion

Teaching is an impossible yet opportunist task. Its success rate is less than 100 per cent, at both the individual and the population level. Parents and schoolteachers wrestle with the eternal search for the one right way. 'Where did I go wrong?'; 'why can't I get it right?'; 'surely, there must be a better way' are their reflections on failure.

In turn, they easily become victims of their own self-examination. Other agencies skilfully trade on these anxieties. The policy context examined in *Rethinking Teacher Education* can be scrutinized against this backdrop. There has been a merging of scapegoats. 'Blame the teacher' is also 'blame the parent'. Schoolteachers and parents are the problem. Teacher education is the remedy, providing the will (and creativity) of teachers can be reduced to certainties.

There is little sense, therefore, of teaching and teacher education as an opportunity. It is no surprise that the social valuation of school teaching and teacher education has slumped. Nor has the monetary valuation (i.e. wage) of schoolteachers counterbalanced the decline in the social valuation of teachers. Both practices, schoolteaching and teacher education, have been reduced to the delivery of deliverables. And deliverance has been reduced to contract compliance in the meeting of targets. Teachers' practice is configured around rule-following under the gaze of centrally imposed criteria, and the resultant achievement of short-term goals.

Little attention is given to the fact that the Enlightenment brought a new democratic agenda to education and schooling, one based more on inclusion, development and potential than upon the identification of performance ceilings, the calibration of competence and the legitimation of differentiation (i.e. exclusion). The pursuit of performativity is to hanker for the certainties of an old premodernist world order. 'Things aren't what they used to be in modern schooling' is the leader-writers' recurrent lament. 'And they never were' is the salutary rejoinder to be found in the deliberations and provocations of *Rethinking Teacher Education*.

Bibliography

Acheson, D. (1998) *Independent Inquiry into Inequalities in Health*: Report. London, Stationery Office.

Anderson, J., Greeno, J., Reder, L. and Simon, H. (2000) 'Perspectives on learning, thinking and activity', *Educational Researcher*, 25:4, 5–11.

Annas, J. and Barnes, J. (1985) *The Modes of Scepticism – Ancient Texts and Modern Interpretations*. Cambridge, Cambridge University Press.

Anning, A. and Edwards, A. (1999) *Promoting Learning from Birth to Five*. Buckingham, Open University Press.

Audi, R. (2001) *The Architecture of Reason: The Structure and Substance of Rationality*. Oxford, Oxford University Press.

Australian Council of Deans of Education (1998) *Preparing a Profession* (Report of the National Standards and Guidelines for Initial Teacher Education Project). Canberra, Australian Council of Deans of Education.

Axel, E. (1997) 'One developmental line in European activity theories', in M. Cole, Y. Engeström and O. Vasquez (eds) *Mind, Culture and Activity*. Cambridge, Cambridge University Press.

Baddeley, A. (1990) *Human Memory: Theory and Practice*. Hillsdale, NJ, Lawrence Erlbaum Associates.

Baker, K. (1987) 'Kenneth Baker looks at future of education system', *DES Press Release*, 9 September.

Barrow, R. (1997) 'Philosophy of education: past, present and future', in D. N. Aspin (ed.) *Logical Empiricism and Post-empiricism in Educational Discourse*. Johannesburg, Heinemann, pp. 69–82.

Bauman, Z. (1993) *Postmodern Ethics*. Oxford, Blackwells.

—— (1997) *Postmodernity and Its Discontents*. Cambridge, Cambridge University Press.

—— (1998) *Work, Consumerism and the New Poor*. London, Open University Press.

Beard, R. (1999) *National Literacy Strategy: Review of Research and Other Related Evidence*. London, DfEE.

—— (2000) 'Research and the national literacy strategy', *Oxford Review of Education*, 26, 421–36.

Benhabib, S. (1992) *Situating the Self*. New York, Routledge.

Bennett, N., Desforges, C., Cockburn, A. and Wilkinson, B. (1984) *The Quality of Pupil Learning Experiences*. London, Lawrence Erlbaum Associates.

Benton, P. (ed.) (1990) *The Oxford Internship Scheme: Integration and Partnership in Initial Teacher Education*. London, Calouste Gulbenkian Foundation.

Berman, M. (1982) *All That Is Solid Melts Into Air: The Experience of Modernity*. London, Verso.

Biggart, N. W. (1989) *Charismatic Capitalism: Direct Selling Organizations in America*. Chicago, University of Chicago Press.

Billig, M. (1987) *Arguing and Thinking: A Rhetorical Approach to Social Psychology*. Cambridge, Cambridge University Press.

Blair, G., Jones, R. S. and Simpson, R. (1954) *Educational Psychology*. New York, Macmillan.

Bloor, D. (1976) *Knowledge and Social Imagery*. London, Routledge & Kegan Paul.

Boaler, J. (1997) *Experiencing School Mathematics: Teaching Styles, Sex and Setting*. Buckingham, Open University Press.

Bottery, M. and Wright, N. (1999) 'The directed profession: teachers and the state in the Third Millennium'. Paper presented to the SCETT Annual Conference, Rugby, 26–8 November.

Bourdieu, P. (1977) *Outline of a Theory of Practice*. Cambridge, Cambridge University Press.

Bridges, D. (1999) 'Educational research: pursuit of truth or flight into fancy?', *British Educational Research Journal*, 25:5, 597–616.

Brown, A. L. (1992) 'Design experiments: theoretical and methodological challenges in creating complex interventions in classroom settings', *Journal of the Learning Sciences*, 2, 141–78.

Brown, J. S., Collins, A. and Duguid, P. (1989) 'Situated cognition and the culture of learning', *Educational Researcher*, 18, 32–42.

Bruner, J. (1996a) 'Frames for thinking: ways of making meaning', in D. Olson and N. Torrance (eds) *Modes of Thought: Explorations in Culture and Cognition*. Cambridge, Cambridge University Press.

—— (1996b) *The Culture of Education*. Cambridge, Mass. Harvard University Press.

Buchberger, F. and Beernaert, Y. (1995) 'Recent developments in teacher-education in the European Union', in T. Sander, F. Buchberger, A. E. Greaves and D. Kallós (eds) *Teacher Education in Europe: Evaluation and Perspectives*. Osnabrück, Ruck-Zuck-Druck, pp. 395–405.

Buchberger, F., Campos, B. P., Kallós, D. and Stephenson, J. (2000) Green Paper on *Teacher Education in Europe: High Quality Teacher Education for High Quality Education and Training*, Umeå, TNTEE Publications (http://tntee.ume.se/publications/greenpaper.html).

Burnet, J. (1905) *Aristotle on Education*. Cambridge, Cambridge University Press.

Campbell, D. T. and Stanley, J. C. (1963) 'Experimental and quasi-experimental designs for research on teaching', in N. L. Gage, *Handbook of Research on Teaching* (pp. 171–246). Chicago, Rand McNally.

Carey, G. (1997) 'Moral values: the challenge and the opportunity'. Opening address to the conference *Values in the Curriculum*, Institute of Education, University of London, 10 April.

Carnegie Corporation of New York (1986) *A Nation Prepared: Teachers for the 21st Century*. New York, Carnegie Corporation of New York.

Carnoy, M. and Castells, M. (1997) 'Sustainable flexibility: a prospective study on work, family and society in the information age'. *OECD Working Papers* V. Paris, OECD.

Carr, W. and Kemmis, S. (1986) *Becoming Critical: Education, Knowledge and Action Research*. London, Falmer Press.

Carter, W. R. and Bahde, J. E. (1998) 'Magical antirealism', *American Philosophical Quarterly*, 35:4, 305–25.

Castells, M. (1997a) *The Power of Identity*. Oxford, Blackwell.

Castells, M. (1997b) *End of Millennium*, volume three of *The Information Age: Economy, Society and Culture*. Oxford, Blackwell.

—— (2000) 'Materials for an exploratory theory of the network society', *British Journal of Sociology*, 51:1, 5–24.

Central Advisory Council for Education (CACE) (1967) *Children and Their Primary Schools (The Plowden Report)*. London, HMSO.

Chaiklin, S. (1993) 'Understanding the social scientific practice of Understanding Practice', in S. Chaiklin and J. Lave (eds) *Understanding Practice: Perspectives on Activity and Context*, Cambridge, Cambridge University Press.

Chaiklin, S. and Lare, J. (eds) (1993) *Understanding Practice: Perspectives on Activity and Context*. Cambridge, Cambridge University Press.

Chalmers, A. F. (1978) *What Is This Thing Called Science?* Milton Keynes, Open University Press.

Chapman, P. (1981) 'Schools as sorters: testing and tracking in California, 1910–1925', *Journal of Social History*, 14, 701–17.

Clark, A. (1997) *Being There: Putting Brain, Body and World Together Again*. Cambridge, Mass., MIT Press.

Clegg, S. C. (1999) 'Globalizing the intelligent organization: learning organizations, smart workers, (not so) clever countries and the sociological imagination', *Management Learning*, 30:3, 259–80.

Cockburn, A. (2000) 'Elementary teachers' needs: issues of retention and recruitment', *Teaching and Teacher Education*, 16, 223–38.

Cole, M. (1995) 'Socio-cultural-historical psychology: some general remarks and a proposal for a new kind of cultural-genetic methodology', in J. Wertsch, P. Del Rio and A. Alvarez (eds).

—— (1996) *Cultural Psychology*. Cambridge, Mass., Harvard University Press.

Cox, C. B. and Dyson, A. E. (eds) (1971) *The Black Papers on Education*. London, Davis-Poynter.

Cuban, L. (1987) 'The Holmes Group Report: why reach exceeds grasp', *Teachers College Record*, 88:3, 348–53.

Dalin, P. and Rust, V. (1996) *Towards Schooling for the Twenty-first Century*. London, Cassell.

Danish Ministry of Education (1999) *The Education of Teachers for the Danish 'Folkskole' at Colleges of Education*. Copenhagen: Laererseminariernes Rektorforsamling.

De Corte, E., Greer, B. and Verschaffel, L. (1996) 'Mathematics teaching and learning', in D. Berliner and R. Calfee (eds) *Handbook of Educational Psychology*. New York, Macmillan.

Department for Education and Employment (1996a) *Press Notice 302/96: 'Shake up of teacher training and new focus on leadership skills for head-teachers – Shephard'* (18 September). London, DfEE.

—— (1996b) Press Notice 255/96: 'Cheryl Gillan addresses Professional Association of Teachers'. London, DfEE.

—— (1997) *Circular 10/97 Teaching: High Status, High Standards*. London, DfEE.

—— (1998) *Circular 4/98 Requirements for Courses of Initial Teacher Training*. London, DfEE.

Department of Education and Science (1984) *Circular 3/84 Initial Teacher Training Approval of Courses*. London, HMSO.

—— (1987) *The National Curriculum 5–16: A Consultation Document*. London, Department of Education and Science.

—— (1992) *Reform of Initial Teacher Training: A Consultation Document 40/92*. London, Department of Education and Science.

Descartes, R. (1637) *Discourse on Method and the Meditations*. Harmondsworth, Penguin (1968).

Desforges, C. (1985) 'Matching tasks to children's attainment', in N. Bennett and C. Desforges (eds) *Recent Advances in Classroom Research*. Edinburgh, Scottish Academic Press.

Doyle, W. (1986) 'Classroom organisation and management', in M. C. Wittrock (ed.) *Handbook of Research on Teaching*, 3rd ed. New York, Macmillan.

Eagleton, T. (2000) *The Idea of Culture*. Oxford, Blackwell.

Edwards, A. (1997a) 'Guests bearing gifts: the position of student teachers in primary school classrooms', *British Educational Research Journal*, 21, 27–37.

—— (1997b) 'Possible futures for initial teacher education in the primary phase', in A. Hudson and D. Lambert (eds) *Exploring Futures in Initial Teacher Education*. London, Bedford Way Papers.

—— (1998) 'Mentoring student teachers in primary schools: assisting student teachers to become learners', *European Journal of Teacher Education*, 21, 47–62.

—— (2001) 'Researching pedagogy: a sociocultural agenda', *Pedagogy, Culture and Society*, 9:2, 161–86.

Edwards, A. and Collison, J. (1995) 'What do teacher mentors tell student teachers about pupil learning?', *Teachers and Teaching: Theory and Practice*, 1, 265–79.

—— (1996) *Mentoring and Developing Practice*. Buckingham, Open University Press.

Edwards, A. and Knight, P. (eds) (1994) *Assessing Competence in Higher Education*. London, Kogan Page.

Edwards, A. and Ogden, L. (1998a) 'Learning in action: learning to teach as participatory appropriation'. Paper presented at the ISCRAT Conference, Aarhus, Denmark.

—— (1998b) 'Constructing curriculum subject knowledge in primary school teacher training', *Teaching and Teacher Education*, 14, 735–47.

—— (1999a) 'Learning to see in classrooms: developing an understanding of the complexity of teaching and learning during initial teacher education'. Paper presented at the AERA Conference, Montreal, Canada.

—— (1999b) 'The missing mentor: a sociocultural analysis of school-based teacher education'. Paper presented at the EARLI Conference, Gothenburg, Sweden.

Edwards, D. (1997) *Discourse and Cognition*. London, Sage.

Elliott, J. (1991) *Action Research for Educational Change* Buckingham, Open University Press.

—— (1993) 'What have we learnt from action research in school-based evaluation?', *Educational Action Research*, 1, 175–86.

Ellis, S. (1997) 'Strategy choice in a sociocultural context', *Developmental Review*, 17, 490–524.

Engeström, Y. (1993) 'Developing studies of work as a test bench of activity theory: the case of a primary care medical practice', in S. Chaiklin and J. Lave (eds) (1993).

—— (1999) 'Innovative learning in work teams: analyzing cycles of knowledge creation in practice', in Y. Engeström, R. Miettinen and R.-L. Punamäki (eds) *Perspectives on Activity Theory*, Cambridge, Cambridge University Press.

Engeström, Y., Brown, K., Christopher, C. and Gregory, J. (1997) 'Coordination, cooperation and communication in the courts: expansive transitions in legal work', in M. Cole, Y. Engeström and O. Vasquez (eds) *Mind, Culture and Activity*. Cambridge, Cambridge University Press.

Engeström, Y., Meittinen, R. and Punamäki, R-L (eds) (1999) *Perspectives on Activity Theory*. Cambridge, Cambridge University Press.

Engeström, Y. and Middleton, D. (eds) (1996) *Cognition and Communication at Work*. Cambridge, Cambridge University Press.

Esping-Anderson, G. (1990) *The Three Worlds of Welfare Capitalism*. Cambridge, Polity.

Farr Darling, L. (2001) 'When conceptions collide: constructing a community of inquiry for teacher education in British Columbia', *Journal of Education for Teaching*, 27:1, 7–21.

Fenstermacher, G. D. (1988) 'The place of science and epistemology in Schön's conception of reflective practice?', in P. P. Grimmett and G. L. Erickson (eds) *Reflection in Teacher Education*. New York, Teachers College Press.

Ferlie, E., Pettigrew, A., Ashburner, L. and Fitzgerald, L. (1996) *The New Public Management in Action*. Oxford, Oxford University Press.

Firestone, W. and Pennell, J. (1997) 'Designing state-sponsored networks: a comparison of two cases', *American Educational Research Journal*, 34, 237–66.

Flew, A. (1976) *Sociology, Equality and Education*. London, Macmillan.

Foucault, M. (1980) *Power/Knowledge: Selected Interviews and Other Writings 1972–77*. Brighton, Harvester Press.

—— (1984) 'What is enlightenment?', in P. Rainbow (ed.) *The Foucault Reader*. London, Pantheon.

Fox, D. and Prilleltensky, I. (eds) (1997) *Critical Psychology: An Introduction*. London, Sage.

Frost, R. (1993) 'Reflective mentoring and the new partnership', in D. McIntyre, H. Hagger and M. Wilkin (1993) *Mentoring: Perspectives on School-based Teacher Education*. London, Kogan Page.

Gage, N. L. (1963) *Handbook of Research on Teaching*. Chicago, Rand McNally.

Galton, M. (1998) 'What do tests measure?', *Education 3–13*, 26:2, 50–9.

Gardner, J. and Oswald, A. J. (1999) 'The determinants of job satisfaction in Britain'. Working Paper, University of Warwick (http://www. warwick. ac. uk/fac/soc/Economics/papers/summg-o. pdf).

Gardner, P. (1993) 'The early history of school-based teacher training', in D. McIntyre, H. Hagger and M. Wilkin (1993) *Mentoring: Perspectives on School-based Teacher Education*. London, Kogan Page.

Garfinkel, H. (1967) *Studies in Ethnomethodology*. Englewood Cliffs, NJ, Prentice-Hall.

Gee, J. P., Hull, G. and Lankshear, C. (1996) *The New Work Order: Behind the Language of the New Capitalism*. St Leonards, NSW, Allen & Unwin.

Gellner, E. (1974) *Legitimation of Belief*. Cambridge, Cambridge University Press.

Gergen, K. (1992) 'Towards a postmodern psychology', in S. Kvale (ed.) *Psychology and Postmodernism*. London, Sage.

Gibbons, M., Limoges, C., Nowotny, H., Schwartzman, S., Scott, P. and Trow, M. (1994) *The New Production of Knowledge*. London, Sage.

Gibson, J. (1979) *The Ecological Approach to Visual Perception*. London, Houghton Mifflin.

Giddens, A. (1990) *The Consequences of Modernity*. Cambridge, Polity Press.

—— (1998) *The Third Way*. Cambridge, Polity Press.

Gilroy, D. P. (1982) 'The revolutions in English philosophy and philosophy of education', *Educational Analysis*, 4:1, 75–91 (reprinted in P. H. Hirst and

P. White (eds) *Philosophy of Education: Major Themes in the Analytical Tradition*, volume 1 of their edited *Philosophy of Education*, London, Routledge, 1998).

—— (1992) 'The political rape of initial teacher training in England and Wales: a JET rebuttal', *Journal of Education for Teaching*, 18, 5–22.

—— (1993) 'Reflections on Schön: an epistemological critique and a practical alternative', in D. P. Gilroy and M. Smith (eds) *International Analyses of Teacher Education*. Oxford, Carfax, pp. 125–42.

—— (1996) *Meaning Without Words: Philosophy and Non-Verbal Communication*. Aldershot, Avebury.

—— (1999) 'New Labour and teacher education in England and Wales: the first 500 days', *Journal of Education for Teaching*, 24:3, 221–9.

Gilroy, D. P. and Wilcox, B. (1997) 'OfSTED, criteria and the nature of social understanding: a Wittgensteinian critique of the practice of educational judgement', *British Journal of Educational Studies*, 45:1, 22–38.

Giroux, H. (1989) *Teachers as Intellectuals*. New York, Bergin & Garvey.

Glennerster, H. (1991) 'Quasi-markets for education?', *The Economic Journal*, 101, September, 1268–76.

Gordon, E. W. (1995) 'Culture and the sciences of pedagogy', *Teachers College Record*, 97:1, 33–46.

Gough, I. (1996) 'Social welfare and competitiveness', *New Political Economy*, 1:2, 209–32.

Grafton, A. and Jardine, L. (1986) *From Humanism to the Humanities: Education and the Liberal Arts in Fifteenth- and Sixteenth-century Europe*. London, Duckworth.

Graham, J. (1998) 'From New Right to New Deal: nationalism, globalisation and the regulation of teacher professionalism', *Journal of In-service Education*, 24:1, 9–29.

Gray, J., Reynolds, D., Fitzgibbon, C. and Jesson, D. (1996) *Merging Traditions: The Future of Research on School Effectiveness and School Improvement*. London, Cassell.

Greeno, J. (1997) 'On claims that answer the wrong questions', *Educational Researcher*, 26:1, 5–17.

Griffiths, A. P. (ed.) (1967) *Knowledge and Belief*. Oxford, Oxford University Press.

Grimmett, P. P. (1988) 'The nature of reflection and Schön's conception in perspective', in P. P. Grimmett and G. L. Erickson (eds) *Reflection in Teacher Education*. Vancouver and New York, Pacific Educational Press and Teachers College Press.

—— (1993) 'Re-visiting collaboration', in D. P. Gilroy and M. Smith (eds) *International Analyses of Teacher Education*. Abingdon, Carfax.

Hager, P. and Peter, M. (eds) (2000) 'Symposium on *Thinking Again: Education After Postmodernism* by Nigel Blake, Richard Smith, Paul Standish and Peter Smeyers', *Educational Philosophy and Theory*, 32:3, 309–49.

Hargreaves, A. (1993) 'Teacher development in the postmodern age: dead certainties, safe simulations and the boundless self?', in D. P. Gilroy and M. Smith (eds) *International Analyses of Teacher Education*. Abingdon: Carfax.

Hargreaves, D. H. (1997) 'A road to the learning society', *School Leadership and Management*, 17:1, 9–21.

Harré, R. (1998) *The Singular Self*. London, Sage.

Harris, B. (1997) 'Repoliticising the history of psychology', in D. Fox and I. Prilleltensky (eds) (1997).

Hartley, D. (1993) 'Confusion in teacher education: a postmodern condition?', in D. P. Gilroy and M. Smith (eds) *International Analyses of Teacher Education*. Abingdon, Carfax.

—— (1997) *Re-schooling Society*. London, Falmer Press.

Hatch, T. and Gardner, H. (1993) 'Finding cognition in the classroom: an expanded view of human intelligence', in G. Salomon (ed.) (1993).

Hatfield, R. C. (1984) 'A role for teacher educators in developing professional knowledge', *Action in Teacher Education*, 6:1–2, 57–62.

Hirst, P. H. (1990) 'Internship: a view from outside', in P. Benton (ed.) *The Oxford Internship Scheme: Integration and Partnership in Initial Teacher Education*. London, Calouste Gulbenkian Foundation.

Hirst, P. and Zeitlin, J. (1991) 'Flexible specialization versus post-Fordism: theory, evidence and policy implications', *Economy and Society*, 20:1, 1–56.

Holmes Group (1986) *Tomorrow's Teachers*. East Lansing, Michigan, The Holmes Group (http://www.udel.edu/holmes/).

—— (1990) *Tomorrow's Schools: Principles for the Design of Professional Development Schools*. East Lansing, Michigan, The Holmes Group (http://www. udel.edu/holmes/).

—— (1995) *Tomorrow's Schools of Education*. East Lansing, Michigan, The Holmes Group (http://www.udel.edu/holmes/).

Huberman, M. 1995 'Networks that alter teaching: conceptualisations, exchanges and experiments', *Teachers and Teaching: Theory and Practice*, 1, 193–211.

IEA (2000) *Third International Mathematics and Science Study (TIMSS), 1999*. TIMSS: Chestnut Hill, Mass., Boston College (http://www.timss.org/ timss1999.html).

Ilon, L. (1996) 'The changing role of the World Bank: education policy as global warfare', *Policy and Politics*, 24:4, 413–24.

Jacques, K. (1998) 'The Teacher Training Agency, higher education and the professionalism of initial teacher educators', in C. Richards, N. Simco and S. Twiselton (eds) *Primary Teacher Education: High Status? High Standards?* London, Falmer.

Johanningmeier, E. (1980) 'American educational research: applications and misapplications of psychology to education', in J. V. Smith and D. Hamilton (eds) *The Meritocratic Intellect: Studies in the History of Educational Research*. Aberdeen, Aberdeen University Press.

Kant, I. (1787) *Critique of Pure Reason*. transl. N. Kemp Smith, 1929. London, Macmillan, 1970.

Kerferd, G. B. (1981) *The Sophistic Movement*. Cambridge, Cambridge University Press.

Koch, S. (1959) 'Epilogue', in S. Koch (ed.) *Psychology: A Study of a Science*, vol. 3. New York, McGraw Hill.

Kogan, M. (1989) 'Accountability and teacher professionalism', in W. Carr (ed.) *Quality in Teaching: Arguments for a Reflective Profession*. Lewes, Falmer, pp. 135–44.

Körner, S. (1974) *Categorial Frameworks*. Oxford, Blackwell.

Kozulin, A. (1996) 'A literary model for psychology', in D. Hicks (ed.) *Discourse, Learning and Schooling*. Cambridge, Cambridge University Press.

Kuhn, T. S. (1970) *The Structure of Scientific Revolutions*, 2nd ed. Chicago, University of Chicago Press.

Kvale, S. (1992) 'Postmodern psychology: a contradiction in terms?', in S. Kvale (ed.) *Psychology and Postmodernism*, London, Sage.

Labaree, D. F. (1992) 'Power, knowledge and the rationalization of teaching: a genealogy of the movement to professionalize teaching', *Harvard Educational Review*, 62:2, 123–54.

—— (1995a) 'Reforming the preparation of teachers: the Holmes Group proposals in *Tomorrow's Schools of Education*'. Paper presented at the PACT conference on *Teachers' Experiences of Educational Reform*, 2–4 April (no location stated).

—— (1995b) 'A disabling vision: rhetoric and reality in *Tomorrow's Schools of Education*', *Teachers College Record*, 97:2, 166–205.

—— (1999) *How to Succeed in School Without Really Trying: The Credentials Race in American Education*. New Haven, Yale University Press.

Lakatos, I. (1970) 'Falsification and the methodology of scientific research programmes', in I. Lakatos and A. Musgrave (eds) *Criticism and the Growth of Knowledge*. Cambridge, Cambridge University Press, pp. 91–196.

Lave, J. (1988) *Cognition in Practice*. Cambridge, Cambridge University Press.

Lave, J. and Wenger, E. (1991) *Situated Learning: Legitimate Peripheral Participation*. Cambridge, Cambridge University Press.

Lawlor, S. (1990) *Teachers Mistaught*. London, Centre for Policy Studies.

Lawton, D. and Chitty, C. (eds) (1998) *The National Curriculum*. London, Institute of Education.

Leach, J. and Moon, B. (eds) (1999) *Learners and Pedagogy*. London, Paul Chapman.

Lewis, C. T. and Short, C. (1969) *A Latin Dictionary*. Oxford, Clarendon Press.

Long, G., MacDonald, S. and Scott, G. (1996) *Child and Family Poverty in Scotland: The Facts*. Glasgow, Save the Children/Glasgow Caledonian University.

Lortie, D. (1975) *Schoolteacher: A Sociological Study*. Chicago, University of Chicago Press.

Luckmann, T. (1982) 'Individual action and social knowledge', in M. Von Cranach and R. Harré (eds) *The Analysis of Action*. Cambridge, Cambridge University Press.

Lukes, S. (1974) 'Relativism: cognitive and moral', *Proceedings of the Aristotelian Society, Supplementary Volume* (reprinted as chapter 8 of his (ed.) *Essays in Social Theory*, London, Macmillan, 1977, pp. 154–74).

Lyotard, J-F. (1979) *The Postmodern Condition: A Report on Knowledge* (trans. G. Bennington and B. Massumi). Minneapolis, University of Minnesota Press.

Macdonald, D. (1999) 'Teacher attrition: a review of the literature', *Teaching and Teacher Education*, 15, 835–48.

McGuffin, P. (1987) 'Mental illness', in R. Gregory (ed.) *The Oxford Companion to Mind*. Oxford, Oxford University Press.

McIntyre, D. (1995) 'Initial Teacher Education as practical theorising: a response to Paul Hirst', *British Journal of Educational Studies*, 43:4, 365–83.

McIntyre, D. and Hagger, H. (1992) 'Professional development through the Oxford Internship Model', *British Journal of Educational Studies*, 40:3, 264–83.

McIntyre, D., Hagger, H. and Wilkin, M. (1993) *Mentoring: Perspectives on School-based Teacher Education*. London, Kogan Page.

McLellan, D. (1977) *Selected Writings of Karl Marx*. Oxford, Oxford University Press.

McNamara, D. (1993), 'Towards re-establishing the professional authority and expertise of teacher educators and teachers', in D. P. Gilroy and M. Smith (eds) *International Analyses of Teacher Education*. Oxford, Carfax, pp. 277–91.

Mahony, P. and Hextall, I. (1997a) *The Policy Context and Impact of the Teacher Training Agency: A Summary of Findings*. London, Roehampton Institute.

—— (1997b) Problems of accountability in reinvented government: a case study of the Teacher Training Agency', *Journal of Education Policy*, 12:4, 267–83.

Mann, H. (1857) *Report of an Educational Tour in Germany, France, Holland, and Parts of Great Britain and Ireland*, 4th ed. London, Simpkin, Marshall and Co.

Martin, B. (1976) 'Review of *Worlds Apart*', *Times Educational Supplement*, 14 January, 20.

Melucci, A. (1996) *The Playing Self: Person and Meaning in the Planetary Society*. Cambridge, Cambridge University Press.

Meyer, J. W., Boli, J., Thomas, G. M. and Ramirez, F.O. (1997) 'World society and the nation-state', *American Journal of Sociology*, 103:1, 144–81.

Miller, A. and Leyden, G. (1999) 'A coherent framework for the application of psychology in schools', *British Educational Research Journal*, 25, 389–400.

Millett, A. (1996) 'Pedagogy: the last corner of the secret garden'. Invited lecture, King's College, London.

Moll, L. (1990) (ed.) *Vygotsky and Education*. Cambridge, Cambridge University Press.

Moll, L. and Greenberg, G. (1990) 'Creating zones of possibilities: combining social contexts for instruction', in L. Moll. (ed.) *Vygotsky and Education*. Cambridge, Cambridge University Press.

Moon, B. (1998) *The English Exception? International Perspectives on the Initial Education and Training of Teachers*. London, UCET.

Moscovici, S. (1998) 'The history and actuality of social representations', in U. Flick (ed.) *The Psychology of the Social*. Cambridge, Cambridge University Press.

National Commission on Excellence in Education (1983) *A Nation at Risk*. Washington, DC, US Department of Education.

—— (1984) *A Nation at Risk: The Full Account*. Portland, Or, USA Research Inc.

Newman, S. (1999) *Philosophy and Teacher Education: A Reinterpretation of Donald A. Schön's Epistemology of Reflective Practice*. Aldershot, Ashgate.

Norman, D. (1978) 'Notes towards a complex theory of learning', in A. Lesgold, J. Pellegrino, S. Fokkema and R. Glaser (eds) *Cognitive Psychology and Instruction*. New York, Plenum.

O'Connor, D. J. (1957) *Introduction to the Philosophy of Education*. London, Routledge & Kegan Paul.

OECD (1998a) *Reforms on Human Resource Management in OECD Countries*. Paris, OECD.

OECD (1998b) *OECD in Figures*. Paris, OECD.

—— (1998c) *Focus On-line: United States*. Paris, OECD.

OECD (1999) *Issues and Developments in Public Management: Survey 1996–1997*. Paris, OECD.

Office for Standards in Education/Teacher Training Agency (1996) *Assessment of Quality and Standards in Initial Teacher Training 1996/97*. London, OFSTED.

OFSTED (1994) *The Handbook for the Inspection of Schools*. London, OFSTED.

Parker, S. (1997) *Reflective Teaching in the PostModern World: A Manifesto for Education in Postmodernity*. Buckingham. Open University Press.

Pea, R. (1993) 'Practices of distributed intelligence and designs for education', in G. Salomon (1993).

Peters, M. (1995) 'Education and the postmodern condition: revisiting Jean-François Lyotard', *Journal of Philosophy of Education*, 29:3, 387–400.

Piaget, J (1970) *The Science of Education and the Psychology of the Child*. New York, Grossman.

Plato, *Theatetus*. trans. F. M. Cornford. London, Routledge and Kegan Paul, 1935.

Polkinghorne, D. (1992) 'Postmodern epistemology of practice', in S. Kvale (ed.) *Psychology and Postmodernism*. London, Sage.

Popper, K. R. (1963) 'Truth, rationality and the growth of scientific knowledge', in his (ed.) *Conjectures and Refutations*. London, Routledge & Kegan Paul, pp. 215–50 (5th ed. 1974).

—— (1970) 'Normal science and its dangers', in I. Lakatos and A. Musgrave (eds) *Criticism and the Growth of Knowledge*. Cambridge, Cambridge University Press, pp. 51–8.

—— (1971) 'Conjectural knowledge: my solution of the problem of induction' (reprinted as chapter one of his *Objective Knowledge*, 1972).

—— (1972) *Objective Knowledge*. Oxford, Oxford University Press.

Postman, N. (1983) *The Disappearance of Childhood*. London, W. H. Allen.

Postman, N. and Weingartner, C. (1969) *Teaching as a Subversive Activity*. Harmonsdworth, Penguin.

Power, M. (1999) *The Audit Society: Rituals of Verification* (2nd ed.). Oxford, Oxford University Press.

Pring, R. (1994) 'The year 2000', in M. Wilkin, and D. Sankey (eds) *Collaboration and Transition in Initial Teacher Training*. London, Kogan Page.

Ravitch, D. (1997) *New Schools for a New Century: The Redesign of Urban Education*. New Haven, Conn., London, Yale University Press.

Resnick, L., Levine, J. and Teasley, S. (eds) (1991) *Socially Shared Cognition*. Washington, American Psychological Association.

Reynolds, D. (1998) 'Teacher effectiveness: better teachers, better schools'. Invited TTA Lecture, London.

Richards, C. (1998) 'Primary teaching: high status? High standards? A personal response to recent initiatives', in C. Richards, N. Simco and S. Twiselton (eds) *Primary Teacher Education. High Status? High Standards?* London, Falmer.

Richards, C., Harling, P. and Webb, D. (1997) *A Key Stage 6 Core Curriculum? A critique of the National Curriculum for Teacher Training*, London, Association of Teachers and Lecturers.

Riley, D. (1983) *War in the Nursery*. London, Virago.

Ritzer, G. (1993) *The McDonaldization of Society: An Investigation into the Changing Character of Contemporary Social Life*. Thousand Oaks, Pine Forge Press.

Roth, T.C. (1972) 'Towards a delineation of professional knowledge', *Kappa Delta Pi Record*, 7:1, 9–1.

Rowland, S. (1987) 'My body of knowledge', *British Journal of In-Service Education*, 13:2, 81–6.

Russell, B. (1918) 'The philosophy of logical atomism', *Monist* (reprinted in R. C. Marsh (ed.) *The Logic of Knowledge*. London, Allen and Unwin, pp. 175–281.

Salomon, G. (1993) *Distributed Cognitions: Psychological and Educational Considerations*. Cambridge, Cambridge University Press.

Sartre, J.-P. (1943) *Being and Nothingness: An Essay in Phenomenology*, trans. H. E. Barnes. London, Methuen, 1969.

Scardamalia, M. and Bereiter, C. (1999) 'Schools as knowledge-building organisations', in D. Keating and C. Hertzman (eds) *Today's Children, Tomorrow's Society: The Development of Health and Wealth of Nations*. New York, Guilford.

Schaffer, H. R. (1996) *Social Development*. Oxford, Blackwell.

Schön, D.A. (1983) *The Reflective Practitioner: How Professionals Think in Action*. New York, Basic Books.

Schön, D.A. and Rein, M. (1977) 'Problem setting in policy research', in C. Weiss (ed.) *Using Social Research in Public Policy Making*. Lexington, D. C. Heath, pp. 235–51.

Schutz, A. (1967) *The Phenomenology of the Social World*. Evanston, Ill., Northwestern University Press.

Scottish Office (1997) *Raising the Standard: A White Paper on Education and Skills Development in Scotland*. London, Stationery Office.

—— (1998) *Scottish Abstracts of Statistics*. Edinburgh, Scottish Office.

Scottish Office Education and Industry Department (1998) *Guidelines for Initial Teacher Education Courses in Scotland*. Edinburgh, Scottish Office.

Scribner, S. (1985) 'Vygotsky's use of history', in J. Wertsch (ed.) (1985).

Seddon, T. (1999) 'A self-managing teaching profession for the learning society?. Paper presented at the *European Conference on Educational Research*, Lahti, Finland.

Seidman, S. (ed.) (1994) *The Postmodern Turn: New Perspectives on Social Theory*. Cambridge, Cambridge University Press.

Sfard, A. (1998) 'On two metaphors for learning and the dangers of choosing just one', *Educational Researcher*, 27:2, 4–13.

Sharan, S. (1980) 'Cooperative learning in small groups: recent methods and effects on achievement, attitudes and ethnic relations', *Review of Educational Research*, 50, 241–71.

Shotter, J. (1993) *Cultural Politics of Everyday Life*. Buckingham, Open University Press.

Shulman, L. S. (1988) 'Schön's gate is square: but is it art?, in P. P. Grimmett and G. L. Erickson (eds) *Reflection in Teacher Education*. New York, Teachers College Press.

Simola, H., Kivinen, O. and Rinne, R. (1997) 'Didactic closure: professionalization and pedagogic knowledge in Finnish teacher education', *Teaching and Teacher Education*, 13:8, 877–91.

Simon, B. (1999) 'Why no pedagogy in England?, in J. Leach and B. Moon (eds) (1999).

Slavin, R. E. (1983) *Cooperative Learning*. New York, Longman.

Smyth, J. (1991) *Teachers as Collaborative Learners*. Buckingham, Open University Press.

—— (ed) (1995) *Critical Discourses on Teacher Development*. London, Cassell.

—— (1998) *Re-making Teaching*. London, Routledge.

South African Government Publication (1996) *An Agenda for Implementing a National Policy on Teacher Supply, Utilization and Development*. Pretoria.

Squirrell, G., Gilroy, P., Jones, D. and Rudduck, J. (1990) *Acquiring Knowledge in Initial Teacher Education: Reading, Writing, Practice and the PGCE Course*. London, British Library and Information Research Report 79.

Sternberg, R. and Horvath, J. (1995) 'A prototype view of expert teaching', *Educational Researcher*, 9–17.

Stigler, S. M. (1999) *Statistics on the Table: The History of Statistical Concepts and Methods*. Cambridge, Mass., Harvard University Press.

Stones, E. (1992a) *Quality Teaching: A Sample of Cases*. London, Routledge.

—— (1992b) 'Alternative scenarios: power and pedagogy'. Discussion paper: *The Second International Colloquium on Teacher Education*, Curia, Portugal, 18–21 June.

Strauss, C. and Quinn, N. (1997) *A Cognitive Theory of Cultural Meaning*. Cambridge, Cambridge University Press.

Taylor, C. (1985) *Human Agency and Language*. Cambridge, Cambridge University Press.

—— (1991) *The Ethics of Authenticity*. Cambridge, Mass., Harvard University Press.

Teacher Training Agency (1997) *Training Curriculum and Standards for New Teachers: Revised Requirements for all Courses of Initial Teacher Training*. London, TTA.

—— (1998) *National Standards for Qualified Teacher Status*. London, Teacher Training Agency.

Thom, D. (1984) 'Intelligence tests and educational reform', in P. Barnes, J. Oates, J. Chapman, V. Lee and P. Czerniewrska (eds) *Personality, Development and Learning: A Reader*. London, Hodder & Stoughton.

Thorndike, E. (1913) *Educational Psychology: The Psychology of Learning*. New York, Teachers College Press.

—— (1932) *The Fundamentals of Learning*. New York, Teachers College Press.

Tochon, F. (2000) 'When authentic experience is "enminded" into disciplinary genres: crossing biographic and situated knowledge', *Learning and Instruction*, 10, 331–59.

Tochon, F., and Munby, H. (1993) 'Novice and expert teachers time epistemology: a wave function from didactics to pedagogy', *Teaching and Teacher Education*, 9, 205–18.

Toulmin, S. (1990) *Cosmopolis: The Hidden Agenda of Modernity*. New York, Free Press.

Trigg, R. (1973) *Reason and Commitment*. Cambridge, Cambridge University Press.

—— (1976) 'Reason, commitment and social anthropology', *Philosophy*, 51, 219–22.

Tulving, E. (1983) *Elements of Episodic Memory*. Oxford, Oxford University Press.

Usher, R. and Edwards, R. (1994) *Postmodernism and Education*. London, Routledge.

Vallicella, W. F. (1984) 'Relativism, truth and the symmetry thesis', *Monist*, 67:3, 452–65.

Valsiner, J. (1998) *The Guided Mind.* Cambridge, Mass., Harvard University Press.

Vygotsky, L. (1987) *The Collected Works of L.S. Vygotsky (Vol. 3). Problems of the Theory and History of Psychology,* edited by R. Rieber and J. Wollcock. London, Plenum.

Walkerdine, V. (1984) 'Developmental psychology and the child-centred pedagogy: the insertion of Piaget into early education', in J. Henriques, W. Hollway, C. Urwin, C. Venn and V. Walkerdine (eds) *Changing the Subject.* London, Routledge.

Watts, D. (1982) 'Can campus-based preservice education survive?, *Journal of Teacher Education,* 33:2, 37–41.

Weiner, B. (1986) *An Attributional Theory of Motivation and Emotion.* New York, Springer Verlag.

Weinert, F. (1984) 'Contra res sempiternas', *Monist,* 67:3, 376–94.

Wells, G. (1999) *Dialogic Inquiry: Toward a Sociocultural Practice and Theory of Education.* Cambridge, Cambridge University Press.

Wells, G. and Chang-Wells, G. L. (1992) *Construction Knowledge Together: Classrooms as Centers of Inquiry and Literacy.* Portsmouth, NH, Heinemann.

Wertsch, J. (1985) (ed.) *Culture, Communication and Cognition.* Cambridge, Cambridge University Press.

—— (1991) *Voices of the Mind: A Sociocultural Approach to Mediated Action.* Cambridge, Mass., Harvard University Press.

Wertsch, J. Del Rio, P. and Alvarez, A. (1995) (eds) *Sociocultural Studies of Mind.* Cambridge, Cambridge University Press.

Westbury, I. and Wilkof, N. (eds) (1978) *Joseph Schwab: Science, Curriculum and Liberal Education.* Chicago, University of Chicago Press.

Whitty, G. (1993) 'Education reform and teacher education in England in the 1990s', in Gilroy and Smith (eds), op. cit., pp. 263–75.

—— (1999) 'Teacher professionalism in new times'. Draft of a paper presented to the SCETT Annual Conference, Rugby, 26–28 November.

Whitty, G., Power, S. and Halpin, D. (1998) *Devolution and Choice in Education: The School, the State and the Market.* Buckingham, Open University Press.

Wilkin, M. (1996) *Initial Teacher Training: The Dialogue of Ideology and Culture.* London, Falmer.

Wilkin, M. (1999) 'The role of higher education in initial teacher education', *UCET Occasional Paper no. 12.* London, UCET.

Wilson, J. (1989) 'De-intellectualisation and authority in education' *Oxford Review of Education,* 15:2, 111–19.

—— (1991) 'Review essay: teacher education (a review of A. Pearson's *Theory and Practice in Teacher Education*), *Oxford Review of Education,* 17:1, 115–21.

Wittgenstein, L. (1921) *Tractatus Logico-Philosophicus,* trans. D. F. Pears and B. F. McGuinness. London, Routledge and Kegan Paul.

—— (1930) 'Remarks on Frazer's *Golden Bough*', *Synthèse*, 1967 (1931–48, reprinted in C. G. Luckhardt (ed.) *Wittgenstein: Sources and Perspectives*, trans. J. Beversluis. Sussex, Harvester Press, 1979, pp. 61–81).

—— (1933) *The Blue and Brown Books* (1933–35). Oxford, Blackwell, 1958.

—— (1949) *On Certainty* (1949–51, eds G. E. M. Anscombe and G. H. von Wright, trans. D. Paul and G. E. M. Anscombe, 1969. Oxford, Blackwell, 1974.

—— (1953) *Philosophical Investigations* (1945–9, trans. G. E. M. Anscombe, 1953. Oxford, Blackwell, 1958).

Index

third way 41–3
Tomorrow's Schools of Education 78, 79
Tomorrow's Schools report 63–7
Tomorrow's Teachers 64, 68
Truth 47–8
TTA (Teacher Training Agency) 72–6

uncertainty 6–7, 137, 140, 141–2; collaborative responses to 101–23;

philosophical 29–52; political and economic 10–28, *see also* certainty
USA 3, 26, 58, 60, 68

Wales 13
websites 117
welfare state 17–22, 27
whole-class teaching 27
willpower 140–2
women 23
world-views 140–2